The Ultimate Guide to Competency Assessment in Healthcare

Second Editon

Donna Wright, RN, MS

*A Creative Healthcare Management Book
published by Professional Education Systems, Inc.*

For permission requests or ordering information, write to:

Creative Healthcare Management
1701 East 79th Street, Suite 1
Minneapolis, MN 55425

or call 1-800-728-7766 or (612) 854-9015 or fax (612) 854-1866

Creative Healthcare Management can also be contacted through e-mail and the internet.

E-mail address: chcm@chcm.com
Internet location: http://www.chcm.com

Professional Education Systems HealthCare Division
200 Spring Street
(800)647-8079
www.pesi.com

Printed in the United States of America.

Library of Congress Cataloging-in-Publication Data
Wright, Donna, 1962–

The Ultimate Guide to Competency Assessment in Healthcare / Donna Wright.

ISBN 1-886624-08-9

Cover design: Professional Education Systems, Inc, and Donna Wright
Page design and composition: MasterProof

This book is dedicated to my sister,
DeAnn Szymonski, who is also a nurse in
healthcare. By sharing her day-to-day triumphs and
challenges, she has helped me see a broader scope
of application for competency assessment.

About the Author

Donna Wright, RN, MS, is a competency and staff development specialist with Creative HealthCare Management in Minneapolis, Minnesota. She received her MS in nursing education from the University of Minnesota. Ms. Wright has helped many healthcare organizations create meaningful, effective competency and staff development programs for all departments. She has published and lectured across the nation on creative educational strategies, self-directed learning, competency assessment and validation, creative approaches to mandatory training, creating a healthy work environment, and implementing shared governance.

Ms. Wright has worked in both staff and leadership roles, and has worked with clinical and nonclinical departments in organizations. Her experiences have taken her to a variety of healthcare settings, including rural Africa. She is a member of the National Nursing Staff Development Organization and received its "Promoting Excellence in Consultation" award in 1995. Ms. Wright is known for her high-energy and refreshing approach to education, competency, and staff development.

*Creative Healthcare Management provides education and consultation on this topic, as well as many others. If you would like to talk with Donna Wright about competency assessment or need help in creating a successful competency assessment program in your organization, feel free to call Creative Healthcare Management at **1-800-728-7766.***

Table of Contents

CHAPTER THREE
Promoting Accountability Through Competency

CHAPTER FOUR

CHAPTER FIVE
Developing a Successful Competency Assessment

CHAPTER SIX

Chapter One

The Goal of Competency Assessment

- What motivates us to engage in competency assessment
- Regulatory standards
- Competency defined

The Goal of Competency Assessment

There are many reasons why an organization may engage in competency assessment. Those reasons may include any or all of the following:

- to evaluate individual performance
- to evaluate group performance
- to meet standards set by a regulatory agency (JCAHO, OSHA, etc.)
- to address problematic issues within the organization
- to enhance or replace performance appraisal

Whatever has led your organization to competency assessment, you should review the intent behind these motivating factors and define why your organization will support and carry out the process of competency assessment.

Competency assessment can take many forms and address multiple needs for your organization. You do not need to be locked into one method of assessment, such as checklists or observer review. This book will explore the factors that may guide your organization's competency assessment process, and a variety of methods you can use to verify identified competencies.

Competency assessment is a fluid, ongoing process. It reflects the skills and abilities needed to carry out any job. Competency assessment helps articulate and evaluate the skills needed to carry out the job *now*, as well as *in the future* as the job evolves over time. For competency assessment to truly be meaningful, it should reflect the dynamic nature of the job. This means you will not have one list of competencies or skills identified for a job that you check off over and over again each year, but instead your competencies will be a collection of skills, abilities, and behaviors that are needed to address the changing nature of the job for a given period of time. These competencies will only be used for that identified assessment period.

Your organization will evolve over time to meet the changing needs and demands of the healthcare environment. Competency assessment is the identification of the specific skills required in each job class to make this organizational evolution successful. It is prudent to clarify with all employees that their jobs will evolve over time as the organization's needs change. No one's job ever stays the same. Through the competency assessment process, the organization is identifying this evolution and inviting the employee to evolve with it.

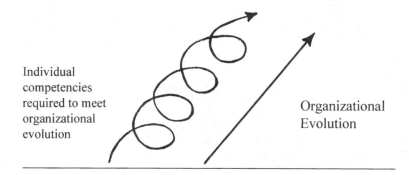

Individual competencies required to meet organizational evolution

Organizational Evolution

The reality is that an organization will never evolve to meet an individual's needs, but individuals are invited to grow and evolve with the organization. The organization must help and support its evolution through education, time, and resources, so the employee can achieve the new skills needed to make this evolution happen. The organization must also realize that if at any time the individual is not comfortable with the direction this organizational evolution is taking, the employee can choose to dissolve his or her contractual agreement with the organization. In other words, employees should make a conscious effort to periodically reflect on their commitment to this organizational evolution—or find an organization to work for that better matches his or her personal philosophies and goals.

Competency assessment can help groups focus on the philosophy and mission of an organization. Competency assessment can also direct employees' participation in and understanding of the identified organizational goals for a given period, as well as help each employee understand and verify his or her contributions to achieving your organizational goals.

Regulatory Standards

Many external regulatory groups dictate the directions we take in our organizations. These groups include the Joint Commission on Accreditation of Healthcare Organizations (JCAHO), the Occupational Safety and Health Administration (OSHA), federal and state standards and licensure boards, and so on.

When planning how to incorporate these standards in our daily operation, we need to consider the intent behind each standard. It is always a good idea to read the regulatory standard for yourself, rather than having someone else summarize it for you. Too many times the meaning of the standards seems to change as one individual passes on his or her interpretation of the standard to the next person.

Understanding the Intent Behind Competency Related Standards

Is the intent behind the standard to provide information or to measure competency?

Providing information:
Many OSHA standards direct us to provide employees with information regarding hazardous materials, so that the employee is informed of the nature of the job and the daily duties. Response to this type of standard may include education, reference material, or mechanisms for getting information from experts if the employee has questions about the nature of the work or substances/equipment used to carry out the work.

Measuring competency:
Many standards, such as the JCAHO standards, require measurement of competency. Competencies are based on organizational performance improvement or quality improvement.

The measurement can take many forms and should be appropriate for the organization's competency definition. Education may be part of the competency process to help the individual achieve the desired competency outcome. Education, in and of itself, is not a measure of competency. In other words, just attending an inservice does not measure competency, unless a competency verification method is incorporated into the class (i.e., case study, return demo, and so on).

Competency Defined

Each organization must write its own definition of competency. Here are a few that may help you get started.

Selected definitions of competency assessment:

- The knowledge, skills, abilities, and behaviors needed to carry out a job.
- Whatever is required to do something adequately. (Pollock, 1981.)
- The ability to perform a task with desirable outcomes under the varied circumstances of the real world. (Benner, 1982.)
- The effective application of knowledge and skill in the work setting. (del Bueno, 1990.)

Keep in mind: If your competency definition requires measurement in real world situations, your competency verification methods should generally reflect this as well.

Your organization should also construct a policy to help guide your competency assessment process. It should include:

- the competency definition
- the process to be used for assessment
- the responsibilities of managers, leaders, educators, and staff in the competency assessment process
- the resources available

Here is a sample of a competency assessment policy:

FORM
Organization-wide
Competency
Assessment
Policy/Procedure

Organization-wide
Competency Assessment
Policy/Procedure

Purpose of competency assessment:

◆ To provide a mechanism for directing and evaluating the competencies needed by our employees to provide quality healthcare services to our customers.

◆ Identify areas of growth and development, and provide opportunities for ongoing learning to achieve continuous quality improvement.

Definition of competency:

Competency is the application of knowledge, skills, and behaviors that are needed to fulfill organizational, departmental, and work setting requirements under the varied circumstances of the real world.

Competency Assessment Process:

Competency assessment will occur on an ongoing basis. Competencies will be identified on an annual basis through a collaborative process, and assessed on a continuum throughout the employment of an individual. This continuum will include assessment during the hire process, initial competencies during the orientation period, and ongoing annual competency assessment.

Hire assessment will include validation of...
* Licensure, registration, and certification (where applicable)
* Previous experience and current skills and abilities through the interview process, reference checking, resumes, and applications.

Initial competency assessment will include validation of...
* Core job functions
* Frequently used functions and accountabilities
* High risk job functions and accountabilities
* Age specific concepts for customers served

Ongoing competency assessment will include validation of...

- New policies, procedures, technologies, and initiatives
- Changing policies, procedures, technologies, and initiatives
- High risk functions and accountabilities
- Problematic job aspects identified (through QI, incident reports, customer surveys, review of aggregate competency data, etc.)

Competency Accountabilities Defined:

The accountability for competency assessment will occur at three levels -- The organizational steering committee for competency assessment, the designated supervisor for each area, and the employee.

The Steering Committee is responsible to...

- Develop a competency definition
- Develop a system for competency documentation
- Provide education and consultation on competency assessment
- Develop organizational competencies
- Develop guidelines and policies for competency assessment
- Develop reporting mechanisms to governing body
- Evaluate competency program

The manager in each area is responsible to...

- Receive and distribute information from the steering group
- Establish a mechanism to identify specific area competencies with staff involvement
- Create an environment that promotes timely competency assessment and ongoing growth and development
- Provide education to employees on the competency process
- Monitor employees progress
- Participate is evaluation of the competency process

The employee is responsible to...

- Complete competencies as indicated
- Participate in competency development
- Participate in evaluation of the competency process

<u>Verification of Individual Competencies</u>:

Each employee will be responsible to complete their own competencies using verification methods they select from an approved list for each competency. The manager's role is to validate at the end of the competency period that the employee has successfully completed this process. The employee will be deemed "competent" with the completion of 100% of the indicated competencies for that job class. If successful completion is not been achieved the employee is "not yet deemed competent," and an action plan is initiated.

Information regarding competency development, verification methods, and competency documentation will be provided in the annual Survival Guide to the Competency Process.

JCAHO definition of competency

"Capacity equals requirement."

| Staff Abilities | $=$ | Organizational Goals/Objectives |

In a nutshell: *Competency assessment should assess, on an ongoing basis, that you have the right staff abilities to carry out your current organizational goals and objectives.*

Competency assessment, and performance improvement in general, will require ongoing assessment and priority setting. The JCAHO performance improvement standards encourage ongoing organizational evaluation and monitoring, and expect that priority setting will be part of that process. We will never be able to address all areas for improvement, but we should be selecting those areas that are of highest concern and have the greatest impact on the services we render to our clients.

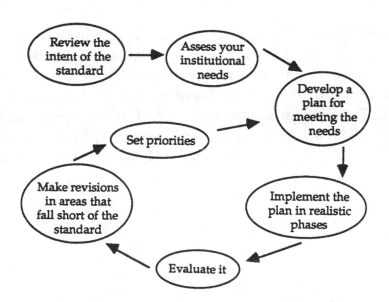

Competency Assessment Is a Continuum

Competency assessment is a fluid, ongoing process. It is dynamic and responsive to the changing environment.

It is not a static process that assesses and re-assesses a list of the same identified competencies year after year.

Most organizations that develop a system that merely checks and re-checks the same list of competencies year after year find their competency assessment process frustrating and meaningless. It can become an overwhelming paper chase. These organizations end up feeling that their competencies do not reflect the current nature of the job classes, and that their competencies frequently need to be revised.

Notes

Notes

Chapter Two

The Essential Elements of Competency Assessment

- Defining the competency continuum
- Assessing all three domains of competency assessment:—technical skills, critical thinking skills, and interpersonal skills
- Developing initial and ongoing competencies for each job class

Competency Assessment Is an Ongoing Process

Employee skills are assessed on a continuum, and are based on the requirements of the job and the ongoing needs of the organization.

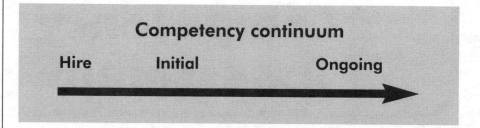

Competency continuum

Hire   Initial   Ongoing

Competencies are assessed when an individual is hired, during the orientation period, and throughout employment as the requirements of the job and the needs of the organization change. Competencies should address the unique needs of each of these periods—Hire, Initial, and Ongoing. You will not have one list of competencies for a job that you check during each of these periods. Instead, you should have dynamic competencies that address each period separately. This is especially true for ongoing competencies.

Keep these things in mind when developing ongoing competencies for each job class:

- Ongoing competency assessment is NOT annual re-assessment of the initial competencies for the job.

- Ongoing competency assessment is a dynamic process that is based on the ever-changing needs required to carry out the organization's mission and goals.

- Ongoing competencies will be different from the initial competencies identified for the job, and will change each competency assessment period.

Hire

Assess competency through . . .

- Licensure
- Registration
- Certification
- Interview questions and checklists
- Previous experience

Initial Competencies

Competencies focus on the knowledge, skills, and abilities required in the first 6 months to a year of employment (the typical time required for orientation and observation prior to independently carrying out the job functions).

Competencies for initial assessment are often referred to as the "core competencies" to perform the job.

Ongoing Competencies

Competencies build on the already established knowledge, skills, and abilities.

Ongoing competencies reflect the new, changing, high-risk, and problematic aspects of the job as it evolves over time.

Assessing All Domains of Skill

Individual job skills will vary from job class to job class. However, these three domains are always present whether you are delivering patient care, tending to the custodial needs of the environment, or providing leadership to the organization.

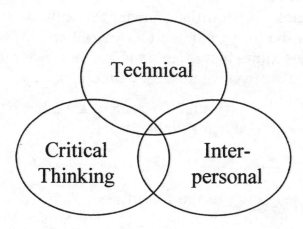

(del Bueno, 1980)

The following are some basic categories in each of the three domains:

Clinical/Technical	Critical Thinking	Interpersonal
• Cognitive skills • Knowledge • Psychomotor skills • Technical understanding (ability to follow directions, carry out procedures)	• Problem solving • Time management • Priority setting • Planning • Creativity • Ethics • Resource allocating • Fiscal responsibilities • Clinical reasoning • Reflective practice • Learning • Change management	• Communication • Customer service • Conflict management • Delegating • Facilitation • Collaborating • Directing • Articulating • Understanding diversity • Team skills

The Key to Meaningful, Cost-Effective Competency Assessment

Quality Improvement

Tying competency assessment to quality improvement is the key to creating meaningful, cost-effective, ongoing competency assessment. Competency assessment should start with your organization's vision and goals. Leadership sets the tone and creates an environment that supports individual accountability for competency assessment. Then ongoing competency assessment and quality improvement efforts must be monitored to help create the skills the organization will need in the future to fulfill its vision and goals.

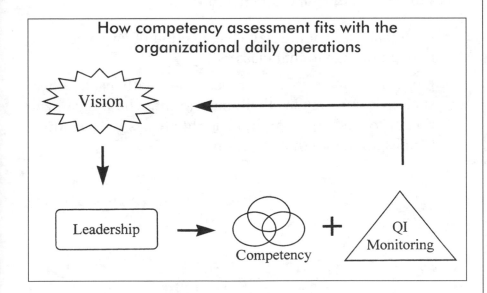

Components of a Successful Competency Assessment Program

The Process Is Consistent but Flexible

- The process has common themes throughout the organization.
- But it is flexible enough to address the needs of individual groups throughout the organization.

The Process Includes Initial and Ongoing Assessment

- Initial competencies address new employee needs.
- Ongoing competencies address the changing nature of the job and the work environment.

The Process Is Specific to Each Job Position

- Each job class should have a collection of competencies that are unique to that class.
- Job groups may share competencies with each other, such as competencies that apply to the whole organization or to a department, but should always have competencies unique to the job group.

Initial Competencies versus Ongoing Competencies

Initial Competencies

Initial competencies are lists of skills needed to get started in a new position. The initial competencies should not be used as a checklist to assess and reassess competencies year after year, because that process does not take into account the changing nature of the work. By using the initial competencies over and over again, you act as if the competencies for any job are static, which in the current reality of healthcare is not true.

When it comes to the skills needed to perform a job, we rarely find that employees lose skills. An employee does not wake up one day and find himself or herself unable to perform a task performed the day before. What more often happens is that the environment or conditions change in relation to that skill, so the employee needs to adapt and advance their skills to meet this need.

Also the assessment and re-assessment can be very costly. Where do you draw the line in the assessment? We could check all sorts of skills needed in the organization, but which skills make a real difference in our service delivery, and which skills have significantly changed, or need to change? Focusing competency efforts on what makes a difference is the key to quality, cost-effective competency assessment.

Tying competency assessment to quality assessment can help your organization identify those skills needed to meet the ever-changing aspects of the healthcare environment—and can prevent you from creating a system that goes beyond what is absolutely needed for each given period. It can also monitor what is truly needed, so that necessary skills and issues are not missed.

Ongoing Competencies

Ongoing competencies need to reflect the changing nature of the job in light of the organizational mission and goals.

When developing ongoing competencies, you should start by assessing the changing nature of the environment. Do not start by merely identifying the important aspects of the job. Although these aspects are essential to the job, they do not necessarily need to be re-assessed after the initial competency assessment, unless they are identified as a changing or problematic part of the job.

Use the *ongoing competency worksheet* to identify the competencies needed for each job for a given period. Brainstorm competency issues for each of the four categories. Then prioritize the issues identified. *The competencies selected should be those skills needed by 100% of the people in that job class.* This is not a list of educational inservice needs, but instead the minimal changing skill sets which are now required for the job. So competencies are the minimal skills needed by all to carry out the current nature of the job.

To make the ongoing competencies meaningful and doable, select around 10 or fewer competencies to focus on for each given assessment period. Organizations are not required to check off every skill needed to carry out a job. Instead, you should focus on the competencies for each job class that most affect your organizational services.

Some groups select too many competencies for a given period. It can be difficult for the employee to accomplish the verification of a large list of competencies in a meaningful way. In these situations, organizations have started out with this large list and were unable to be complete them. So a secondary, condensed version of the competencies is often substituted half way through the year. This approach leaves bitter feelings about the competency process for both staff and managers. It also undermines the overall philosophy of the competency assessment process.

When developing your competency list for each job class, try to keep it something that is achieveable. I recommend 10 or fewer competencies every year (or whatever time period you select.) Use the ongoing competency worksheet to prioritize the competencies from the items you have identified.

Establishing an environment of success, especially in the early development of your competency assessment process, will create an environment of acceptance and buy-in to the process. When the competency process is viewed as meaningful to the employees and helps guide them in achieving the organization's goals for the year, you will build more collaborative teams and departments.

Competency Development

Initial competencies reflect the knowledge, skills, and behaviors required in the first six months to a year in a particular job class. This usually is defined by the indicated probation period of the job.

Develop initial competencies based on:

- Core job functions
- Frequently used job functions and accountabilities
- High-risk* job functions and accountabilities

Ongoing competencies reflect the periodic assessment of employees in a job class after the initial competencies have been met. The assessment period is determined by the organization.

Develop ongoing competencies based on:

- New initiatives, procedures, technologies, policies, or practices
- Changes in procedures, technologies, policies, or practices
- High-risk* job functions and accountabilities
- Problematic areas identified by QI data, patient surveys, staff surveys, incident reports, or any other evaluation processes—whether formal or informal

---

*High-risk refers to anything that would cause harm, death, or legal action to customers, employees, or the organization.

Worksheet for Identifying Ongoing Competencies

Job Class _____ *Dept./Area*_____ *Date* _____

Step 1: Brainstorm staff needs in each of the categories listed below.

Step 2: Prioritize those needs and choose which ones the organization will focus on.

Competency Needs:	*Priority:* *Hi - Med - Lo*
What are the NEW procedures, policies, equipment, initiatives, etc. that affect this job class	
What are the CHANGES is procedures, policies, equipment, initiative, etc. that affect this job class.	

What are the HIGH RISK aspects of this job. *High risk is anything that would cause* **harm**, **death**, *or* **legal action** *to an individual or the organization.*	
What are PROBLEMATIC aspects of this job. *These can be identified through quality management data, incident reports, patient surveys, staff surveys, and any other form of evaluation (formal or informal)*	

Reminder: *Are there any age-specific aspects in any of the priority areas listed above? Add age specific aspects to a competency selected above rather creating a separate age specific competency.*

Try to limit your focus to no more than 10 competencies each year. Trying to focus on more than that can be confusing and overwhelming for both staff and leaders.

Notes

Notes

Chapter Three

Promoting Accountability Through Competency Assessment

- Defining accountabilities for employees and managers
- Competency assessment forms that promote individual accountability
- Documenting competency assessment
- Examples of how to develop competencies that reflect your organizational needs

Accountability

Both the employees and leadership have accountabilities in the competency assessment process. These accountabilities should be stated clearly in your competency policy and articulated to both management and staff throughout your organization.

Defining Accountability during the Hire Process

Competency expectations should be articulated not only to current employees but also to new hires. Articulating these expectations before the person accepts the job can help promote acceptance and growth of the competency expectations within the organization. I include a statement in letters I send out to potential new employees that reflects this competency expectation. I usually add something like this to the letters I send out to new hires stating that they have the job if they would like to accept it:

> Upon acceptance of this job, you are expected to participate in our ongoing competency assessment process. As the organization grows and evolves, so will the activities needed in your job. We will help you evolve the ongoing skills you will need along the way and we invite you to share in this process. Participation in the competency process is a requirement for every employee in our organization. If you would like more information about our competency assessment process or any other aspects of the job, please feel free to contact me.

Incorporating Accountability into Your Overall Competency Process

A competency assessment philosophy that helps clarify and articulate accountability is shown in the following model:

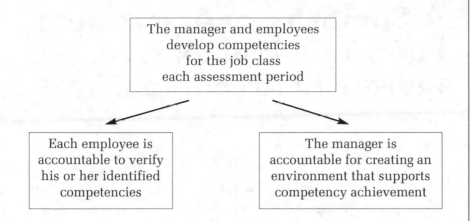

The employee is accountable to verify his or her own identified competencies. This does not mean that the employee does a self assessment. It does, however, mean that the employee must collect the evidence that demonstrates individual competency. This puts ownership of competency assessment on each individual in the organization, and takes the manager out of the role of observer and evaluator. Most managers and supervisors take on the role of evaluator of employee performance, when in fact most managers are not in the position to truly evaluate day-to-day competencies. The manager's role should be to establish systems that support competency assessment and guide this process—not to do the assessment for the employee. By adopting this philosophy, you will not only promote accountability in the employees, but you will be able to utilize your managers in more productive roles, such as coach and facilitator. This will help managers truly "manage" and hold employees accountable.

A Competency Assessment Form That Promotes Individual Accountability

The format you use to articulate and track competency assessment can also be the tool you use to promote individual accountability. The following pages show one example of a format that helps articulate to the employee the identified competencies for a given period and the approved method the employee may select to verify the identified competencies.

Here is an example of one competency statement and several verification methods that can validate the competency listed. These statements can be inserted into the competency form on page 36. The employee is then able to choose from the verification methods listed. All of these methods can demonstrate skills in customer service. By allowing the employee to select the verification method, you give the employee some ownership in the process.

Competency Example

Competency Statement

Demonstrates the ability to apply customer service principles to everyday work situations.

Verification Methods

❑ Submit two customer services peer reviews completed by two different coworkers.

❑ Submit one customer service exemplar based on information from a patient/family member. May include cards, letters, or patient satisfaction information that identifies you by name.

❑ Participate in a case study/discussion group session on customer service.

❑ Complete two customer service case studies.

This type of competency assessment process holds the employee accountable for his or her competency assessment. Therefore, the employee is responsible for initiating the competency assessment validation. The manager's role is then to create an environment that encourages and supports this achievement, rather than to "check off' or observe the employee's behavior. For example, the manager may identify "customer service" as the competency for the month. The manager can set up the case study/discussion group activities for that month and other activities that support the competency assessment of that skill. This will encourage the employee to participate. If the employee chooses not to participate that month, his or her options will be fewer later on. This is a great way to reward the behavior of motivated employees. Too many times our competency programs only focus on poor performers. By offering multiple choices early in the assessment period, you will be offering motivated employees a greater variety of choices.

If an employee chooses not to do the competency at all, he or she will not be "deemed competent." Your organizational policies should articulate the range of consequences for not completing competency assessment as indicated. A good way to develop these types of strategies (or consequences) is to have discussions with other managers about possible responses to different situations. Discuss your "what if this happens" situations. Describe your worst employee nightmares. By discussing these scenarios before they happen, you will begin to see a variety of creative options that can be applied to the variety of situations you will face as managers. Chapter 5 will discuss this topic of consequences further.

Documenting Competency Assessment

The role of the manager, at the end of the competency period, is not necessarily to verify the employee's skill, but to determine if the employee has successfully completed the identified verification methods. The manager then indicates that the employee is **"competent,"** because the employee has successfully completed all the identified competencies, or **"not yet deemed competent,"** which indicates the identified competencies have not been completed.

The label "not yet deemed competent" reflects many circumstances that may be seen in the competency assessment process:

- completing some, but not all, of the competencies identified
- leaves of absence
- procrastination or resistance to participating in the competency process

If the employee is *not yet deemed competent,* an action plan must be indicated in the employee's record somewhere. This action plan should include the actions to be taken by the employee and manager, and a time for when these actions will be reviewed.

The following pages give one example of a competency form that can articulate the competency expectations for a given time period and promote employee accountability. The first step in the process is to identify the competency priorities for the time period by using the *ongoing competency assessment worksheet* in Chapter 2. Then write competency statements that reflect the skills identified.

This form uses the skill domains developed by del Bueno (1980) to categorize the competencies identified into the three skill areas: technical, critical thinking, and interpersonal. This is not a requirement in the competency process but does create a healthy balance in the skill assessment.

Once the competencies are identified, you can begin to develop or identify ways to verify the competency statements. This does *not* need to be an observation through a checklist. There are 11 different verification methods. These methods are presented in Chapter 4, along with examples of each. You will want to select the verification methods that best reflect the competency skill identified for each competency statement. You will **never** want to use just one verification method to meet all the competencies identified for a given period. No single verification method can truly measure all the areas of competency assessment—technical, critical thinking, and interpersonal. So avoid creating one method that you insert the competencies into every year for verification—such as a checklist.

In addition, I encourage you not only to select different verification methods for the competencies identified, but to offer more than one verification option for *each* competency statement. This way you provide the employee with choices. This strategy will increase ownership in the process as the employee selects his or her preference from one of the verification methods identified on the form.

FORM
Competency
Assessment

Competency Assessment Form for _____

(competency assessment period)

Name _____　　　　Job Class _____　　　　Work Area _____

This form is to be completed by the employee. For each of the competency statements listed below, the employee may select which method of verification method they would like to use to validate their skill in that area. See the method of verification for details on completion. When this form is complete submit it to the area supervisor as indicated.

Competency	Method of Verification	Date Completed
Technical Domain		
Critical Thinking Domain		
Interpersonal Domain		

The following are a list of the annual training required for this job class. Select one of the Method of Education that you prefer.

Annual Retraining	Method of Education	Date Completed

This section to be completed by supervisor:

With consideration of the employees performance and competency assessment, this employee is competent to perform as a/an _____ on/in _____.

☐ **Yes**   ☐ **No** (Not yet deemed competent)

Action Plan:

Employee Signature _____ Date _____   Supervisor Signature _____ Date _____

On the following pages you will find an example of an actual competency form developed for the job class of ER Telephone Triage Nurse. Two nurses within the job class of Telephone Triage Nurses and the manager for these nurses sat down together to develop these competencies for the year. They used the *Worksheet for Identifying Ongoing Competency* found on pages 25 and 26 to identify and select the competencies listed. These selected competencies reflect the new, changing, high risk, and problematic aspects of the current job and the needs of the organization.

This group selected seven competencies for the year. They reflect the following aspects of the job:

- Problematic aspect of **documentation** reflected in quality improvement monitors data collected throughout the year

- New patient population of **eating disorder patients**

- New equipment—new complex **telephone system**

- Change in **organizational care delivery** approach— Primary Nursing

- New managed care environment (and **decision-making** related to this changing environment)

- Problematic aspect of **customer service** hospital-wide that was identified though patient satisfaction surveys

- The second phase of a hospital-wide initiative **healthy work environment**

Once the competencies were identified, then verification methods were created to reflect each competency. Several verification methods were created for each competency to give employees a choice. Verification methods were chosen that would truly capture the nature of the competency, but that would also allow easy verification for motivated employees or for employees who already have the skills identified for the current nature of the job.

FORM

Sample
Competency
Assessment Form
for ER Telephone
Triage Nurse

Competency Assessment Form for ER Telephone Triage Nurse

Name _____ Job Class _____ Work Area _____

This form is to be completed by the employee. For each of the competency statements listed below, the employee may select which method of verification method they would like to use to validate their skill in that area. See the method of verification for details on completion. When this form is complete, submit it to the area supervisor as indicated.

Competency	Method of Verification	Date Completed
Technical Domain		
Documentation: Regularly uses evaluative statements in charting progress to meet cutcomes identified for the patient	☐ Submits two copies of charting that reflects evaluative statements ☐ Attend charting inservice and complete case studies in the class	
Eating Disorder Patient Support: Demonstrates a basic understanding of crisis intervention for eating disorder patients and appropriate interventions to use with these crisis calls.	☐ Attend the inservice on "The Basics of Eating Disorders" and complete the case study packet ☐ Complete the Eating Disorder Case Study Packet ☐ Completes the Eating Disorder Self Learning Packet and Exam	

Telephone System:
Demonstrates the ability to use the new phone system -- including voice mail, conference calling, and call back features.

- ☐ Return demonstration in telephone class
- ☐ Peer/Supervisor observation of using the new phone system _____
  Observers signature

Critical Thinking Domain

Care Delivery Initiative: *(Primary Nursing Implementation)*
Understands and actively supports the new care delivery models adopted by the organization -- Primary Nursing

- ☐ Complete the Primary Nursing Exemplar
- ☐ Attend one of the Primary Nursing Focus groups (see newsletter for dates/times)

Problem-solving and care decisions in managed care:
Demonstrates an understanding of resources and options available to patients as the healthcare environment changes to managed care

- ☐ Participate in the ER Managed Care discussion groups
- ☐ Give a presentation on the options available through the various managed care providers and lead one of the discussion groups

Interpersonal Domain

Customer Service:
Demonstrates the application of customer service principles into the work setting

- ☐ Compile two "Customer Service Peer Reviews" from peers or patient/family members
- ☐ Complete the "Customer Service Exemplar"

Healthy Work Environment: (Phase 2)
Actively participates in creating a healthy work environment as reflected in the Commitment to my Coworker card and Healthy Work Environment policies

- ☐ Participates in one of the team face-to-face peer review sessions
- ☐ Participates in the written peer review process

This section to be completed by supervisor:

With consideration of the employees performance and competency assessment, this employee is competent to perform as a/an _____ on/in _____ .

☐ **Yes**　　☐ **No** (Not yet deemed competent)

Action Plan:

Employee Signature _____ Date _____ Supervisor Signature _____ Date _____

Notes

Notes

Competency Assessment Verification Methods

- Go beyond checklists
- Explore 11 different ways to verify competencies
- Discover verification methods that can measure critical thinking and interpersonal skills

Verifying Competency

Competency verification methods are used to measure the abilities of an individual for a specific competency statement.

Competency verification methods include: Post-tests, return demos, observation, case studies, exemplars, peer review, self assessment, discussion groups, presentations, mock events, and QI monitors.

Competency verification can *and should* take many forms within the overall competency process. A single method of verification can never effectively capture all three of the domains (technical, critical thinking, and interpersonal). Therefore a variety of methods should be used to assess the competency statements articulated.

- Do you currently use a collection of checklists to assess all your competencies?

- Do most of your competency verification methods address only the technical domain of the job?

- Do you wish you could assess more aspects of critical thinking and interpersonal skills?

If you answered "yes" to any of these questions, this chapter will offer you some other options to help you create a competency program that can more accurately assess the skills of the employees in your organization. This chapter describes 11 different verification methods. Some verification methods are better for measuring technical skills, some are better for critical thinking skills, and yet others will help you measure interpersonal skills. There is no **one** verification method that can measure all three skill domains, so you should always use a variety of verification methods in your competency assessment.

To measure all the domains of skill required to carry out a job, you need to go beyond checklists and post-tests.

- Checklists (observations of skills) are appropriate to measure the technical ability to carry out a procedure.

- Post-tests can measure the knowledge base individuals possess on a given concept.

- Checklists and post-tests are often unable to measure critical thinking or interpersonal abilities.

- Not every competency can be observed by an observer (which is the basic premise for the checklist process).

- Some competencies require a reflection of actions taken. Some even require reflection of the choice "not to act" (in situations where not acting was the competent action). Verification methods like exemplars, case studies, peer review, self assessment, and discussion groups can facilitate the assessment of these types of competencies.

Competency Verification Continuum

The different competency verification methods can be placed along a continuum. Measuring basic skills and knowledge are on the left side of the continuum and reflection of actions falls on the right side of the continuum. Measurement of technical skills can often be done by using methods that fall on the left end of the continuum. Critical thinking and interpersonal skills can be measured by methods that use reflection of actions on the right end of the continuum.

Competency Verification Continuum

Measurement of basic skills/ knowledge	Measurement through reflection of actions

• Factual	• Contextual
• Usually only one answer acceptable	• Expect a variety of answers
• Educator as transmitter of knowledge	• Educator as coach

(Reed & Procter, 1993)

We are sometimes not as comfortable with verification methods on the right end of the continuum. These methods rely more on contextual descriptions of performance rather than factual, one-right-answer approaches. Reflections of actions do not rely on a score or number to measure the outcome, but rather written or verbal descriptions of intended outcomes.

Adult Learning Concepts

The most successful competency programs have a strong foundation in adult learning principles. By building your program on adult learning principles, you create a program that supports accountability in employees and respects the employees' freedom to express individuality in the process.

One key in creating accountability and ownership in the competency process is to give people choices in how they carry out the competency assessment process. People have more buy-in to the process if they have some control over the options they can choose from within the process.

Many of the competency and educational approaches in our organizations rely on the educational concepts we were exposed to as children. Adult learning principles take a slightly different approach. These principles focus on the aspects that motivated adult learners. Below is a summary of the adult learning principles described by Malcolm Knowles (1988). These principles can be used in your educational activities, as well as in the competency assessment process.

Adult Learning Principles
(Knowles)

- Articulate to the learner why he or she needs to know a given skill or information
- Build on the learner's experiences
- Encourage the sharing of experiences
- Provide real-life situations as examples, or have the learner provide them
- Allow sufficient time for learning
- Provide a variety of learning methods

- Use a task-oriented, problem-solving approach to learning

- Use self-directed learning as a learning option when possible

Incorporating these adult learning principles into your competency program can help create a successful program. Discussions should begin with those individuals who share responsibility for administering your competency assessment program—managers, educators, and human resources personnel.

Discuss what outcomes you desire in your overall competency efforts. Discussing these outcomes can help provide consistency throughout the organization, but still allow individual groups to add specific details to create a program that meets their unique issues. Identifying these characteristics of your competency program will also help you develop criteria that can be used to periodically evaluate your competency program.

Strong competency programs share these general characteristics:

- An emphasis on outcomes or achievement of performance expectations

- Flexibility and time allowed for achievement of outcomes

- Use of self-directed learning activities

- Assessment of previous learning

- Use of educator as facilitator/resource

- Incorporation of various learning styles

Competency Verification Methods

There are 11 different competency verification methods. Each verification method will capture different aspects of the job—technical, critical thinking, and interpersonal skills. No *one* verification method can assess all three of these skill domains. To truly assess all aspects of the job, you must use a variety of competency verification methods.

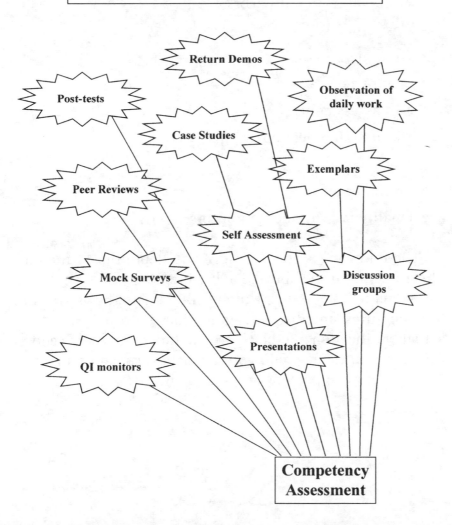

Methods of Competency Verification

Return Demos

Post-tests

Observation of daily work

Case Studies

Exemplars

Peer Reviews

Self Assessment

Mock Surveys

Discussion groups

Presentations

QI monitors

Competency Assessment

After you identify the competency needs for a job class for your current competency assessment period (see workshop for identifying ongoing competencies on pages 25 and 26), then select verification methods that will capture the type of skill you have identified. Providing several verification methods that measure the competency is even better. Offering employees several ways to verify their competencies will provide choices to the employees. This approach builds adult learning concepts into your competency program and creates ownership in the competency process.

The 11 different verification methods are listed below:

- Post-tests
- Return demonstrations
- Observation of daily work
- Case studies
- Exemplars
- Peer review
- Self assessment
- Discussion/reflection groups
- Mock events
- Presentations
- Quality improvement monitors

The following sections describe in detail the 11 methods of verification listed above. Each section describes the verification method, identifies which skill domain the verification best measures, and discusses guidelines for use. Examples of actual verification methods are included in each section. These examples may help you to create verification methods to meet your competency assessment needs.

Post-Tests

Post-tests work well to measure cognitive skills in the technical domain.

Post-tests include a variety of methods that measure attainment of cognitive information. Written tests, quizzes, oral exams, surveys, worksheets, calculation tests, crossword puzzle tests, and some forms of gaming can all reflect the principles behind post-test evaluation.

Although post-tests do a good job of measuring cognitive skills, post-tests generally do not reflect the behavioral, performance, or psychomotor skills of an individual. Post-tests are great to measure an individual's comprehension of basic knowledge related to a particular topic, or to determine if problems can be cognitively processed using given formulas or algorithms (for example, medication calculations). Post-tests have difficulty measuring behavioral skills such as critical thinking or interpersonal skills. Post-tests cannot generate the realities of the real world that truly influence the behaviors associated with these skills—skills such as dealing with a difficult customer. You may ask an individual to select the correct response to a situation with a difficult customer from a list of answers. The individual may answer this question right 100% of the time, but may still be unable to carry this action out effectively in a real-world situation.

So, post tests have their place in validating competency when the desired outcome of the assessment is a measurement of cognitive knowledge and skill. Just keep in mind that this method is limited to the validation of cognitive retention of information. Ask yourself the question, "Is retention of information the outcome we want to achieve for this competency?" If the answer is yes, then post-tests are a good choice. However, be aware that sometimes post-tests are used because we like to feel that we have a concrete way of measuring something. Having a score or numerical value often gives us a sense of security in our measurement of a competency. Do not be deceived by this false sense of security. And avoid the trap of feeling that a number is the only way to justify a competency. Competency can be measured many different ways—and should be measured many different ways. And a numerical score may not always be applicable or required.

A common question I am asked related to the use of post-tests is, "What is an acceptable passing score for a post-test—75%, 80%, 90%?" My answer is generally this: "It depends on the questions you ask in your post-test." I do not have a percentage that I use for all tests. For example, if you have a test with 10 questions and the test taker gets questions 1–9 right, he or she would have a score of 90%. The test taker failed to answer question number 10 correctly. What if question number 10 covered something that, if not done correctly, could kill someone? Then would a score of 90% be acceptable? I think most of us would be uncomfortable with that test outcome. So I generally define test scoring parameters based on the relevance of the questions to the outcomes I am trying to achieve. Sometimes I require a score of 100% as the minimum score for a test. Sometimes I have a combination of parameters. For example, I may require a score of 85% or higher on questions 1–9, and question 10 must be answered correctly (100%) because it involves a life-or-death situation. Make your own judgment for each post-test based on the overall outcomes you are trying to achieve.

So when you identify a competency that requires an outcome of the retention or understanding of information, a post-test is a great way to validate this type of skill. But remember, post-tests have their limitations as a competency verification method. So use them wisely.

Be Aware of the Chemicals you work with...

The following new product is now available on our cleaning carts as a multi-surface cleaner. Understanding this product will help us provide a safe environment for our customers and ourselves.

Clean-ALL

Test what you know about this new product

Refer to HazMat Reference Book for answers. Answers also posted on Safety Bulletin Board.

What is it? Clean-ALL is a germicidal detergent used to clean surfaces in patient care areas and public spaces.

How is it harmful? Clean-ALL may cause _____ irritation.

What special protection do I need to work with this substance? Wear _____ whenever using this product. Clean-ALL can cause skin irritations for some people.

What should I do if I am exposed to this substance? For Eyes.
Flush for _____ minutes, and seek medical attention.

If Swallowed:
Drink a large glass of _____. Call a doctor.
Do not induce vomiting.

New Product Review : Clean-ALL
This section must be completed and returned to the Safety Committee, Box 2124, Hospital Mail.

Check one:

❏ I have completed the safety worksheet on new chemical and have no further questions at this time.

❏ I have completed the safety worksheet, but have further questions. Please contact me at
_____. (You will be contact by the Safety Officer or committee member within 72 hours)

Employee signature _____ Date _____

Diabetes Mellitus Cross Word Puzzle

Across

5. This is an important component in maintaining good control of diabetes.

6. The type of insulin that peaks in 6-10 hours and lasts at least 18 hours.

8. This can happen to tissue if injection sites are not rotated.

Down

1. Sign of this include: nausea, vomiting, weakness, lethargy, headaches, heavy breathing, abdominal pain and high blood glucose levels.

2. Insulin absorption will _____ according to the injection site chosen.

Across

11. You do not do this to the site after an insulin injection.

12. This type of hemoglobin test shows how well diabetes has been controlled over a 2-3 month period.

14. Used to treat an unconscious person with diabetes.

16. Always check this date on the insulin bottle.

17. What the body breaks down when glucose is not available for cell energy.

18. A diabetic should carry some form of this with them at all times.

20. When insulin is not available or working as it should, _____ cannot enter the muscle cells, and builds up in the blood stream.

21. A sign of hyperglycemia.

22. This urine test should be done anytime the blood glucose is greater than 300, if the patient feels sick or has signs of hyperglycemia.

Down

3. This needs to be known, specified, ordered, about the type of insulin the patient takes before administering any insulin. It is another name for source.

4. This should be assessed on a daily basis at home and in the hospital.

7. When a long and short acting insulin are given at the same time, this one is drawn up first.

9. The frequency with which patients should record blood glucose levels, insulin taken and reactions.

13. Illness usually _____ (increase or decrease) the blood glucose level.

15. A sign of hypoglycemia.

19. The species of insulin or insulin source most used.

Bonus Questions

23. When glucose cannot enter the muscle cells and builds up in the blood stream, what condition is the result?

24. Exercise _____ (increases or decreases) need for insulin, when the beginning blood glucose level is < 240.

25. Name the insulin site which is to be used for most patients ≥ 6 years of age.

Diabetes Mellitus Cross Word Puzzle Answers

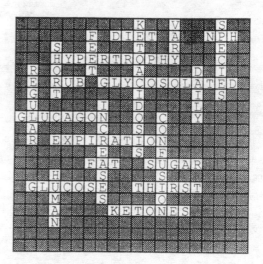

Bonus Answers

23. Hyperglycemia

24. Decreases

25. Abdomen

Managers Competency
Understanding the Americans with Disabilities Act

Competency Post-test Validation

Competency :

Demonstrates an understanding of the Americans with Disabilities Act, and its application to the work setting.

The answers can be found in the ADA Managers Guide available from Human Resources or by attending one of the ADA workshops offered this year (see the hospital newsletter for dates and locations of the classes). Information on the ADA can also be found on the internet. (http://www.usdoj.gov/crt/ada/qandaeng.htm)

1). The Americans with Disabilities Act generally states that disabled persons are entitled to... _____

_____

_____

_____

_____

2). An employer may <u>not</u> ask or require a job applicant to take a medical exam before making a job offer, or make any inquiries about the nature or severity of the disability. However, the employer <u>can</u> ask an individual what two things?

   a)

   b)

3). List 3 reasonable accommodations employees with disabilities may need the employer to make:

a)

b)

c)

4). When is an employer required to make a reasonable accommodation?

Answers to Managers ADA Post-test:

1) … equal opportunities in public accommodations, employment, transportation, state and local government services, and telecommunications. It gives civil rights protection to individuals with disabilities similar to those provided to individuals based on race, color, sex, national origin, age, and religion.

2) a. About the ability the individual has to perform specific job junctions

   b. Ask an individual with a disability to describe or demonstrate how he/she would perform particular job functions.

3) -- making existing facilities used by the employees readily accessible or usable by an individual with a disability.

   -- restructuring the job

   -- modifying work schedules

   -- acquiring or modifying equipment

   -- modifying exams, training, or other programs

4) When the disability becomes "known" to the employer. This is usually triggered by a request from the individual with the disability.

For more details about the above answers refer to the resources mentioned on the top of the ADA Competency Post-test.

Return Demonstration

Return demonstrations are great for measuring technical skills.

A return demonstration involves an individual demonstrating a set of skills to another skilled observer. Return demonstrations may occur in an artificial environment such as a skills lab or classroom, or they may also occur in a real-world setting. Return demonstrations, whether done in an artificial environment or real-world setting, always have one thing in common—there is a **"control factor."** In an artificial setting, the control factor is the setting itself. You are removing the employee from the public setting and allowing for possible mistake-making to occur.

In a real-world setting, where the skill is being performed in public or on a patient, the control factor becomes the observer of the return demonstration. The observer must be aware of this role of being the "control factor." The duty of the observer is to keep the environment safe. He or she must stop the skill demonstration any time the skill is not being performed in a safe manner or has negative consequences for the patient, public, or employees.

Return demonstrations are usually a planned activity in which the individual is asked to demonstrate his or her skills for the purpose of assessment. Return demonstrations are excellent for verifying competencies that require psychomotor skills. Describing an action is one thing; doing it is quite another. To proficiently and accurately carry out some job functions may require a return demonstration of that ability.

Examples of skills for which a return demonstration would be an appropriate verification method include:

Clinical:

- Airway bagging techniques
- IV starting skills

- Fingersticking skills
- Lab tests
- Suturing and suture removal
- X-ray procedures
- Cardiopulmonary resuscitation (CPR) procedures

Non-clinical:

- Operating certain types of cleaning equipment (environmental services)
- Demonstrating a restraining hold on a violent individual (security officers)
- Following a recipe or meal preparation plan (dietary/food services)

A few things to keep in mind:

- Make sure the observers are using a standard set of guidelines or criteria for evaluation. This can be done by using a checklist *or* by simply using already identified policies for the procedure. Whatever format you choose, make sure that the observer is aware of the criteria for evaluation and their role in the process. Articulating this expectation to the observers will assure uniform evaluation, and discourage evaluation based on individual preference.

- Use return demonstration in a real-world setting only if it will not harm or interfere with patient outcomes.

- Return demonstrations can be done immediately following an educational event or instruction, or they can be done at a later time. It is perfectly OK to ask the individual to initiate the return demonstration and seek out the appropriate observer later in a real work situation. This promotes accountability in individuals by asking them to carry out the verification process. (See the verification tool on page 67 for an example of this approach.)

Return demonstrations are an excellent way for an observer to evaluate the technique of the individual. Job functions requiring the proficient use of psychomotor skills can easily and accurately be evaluated using this verification method. Return demonstrations, whether done in an artificial environment or real-world setting, do not capture certain behavioral and attitudinal responses. For example, you may be able to assess the CPR techniques of an individual, but not the timely response to an emergency or any emotional responses that may cause him or her to be unable to perform appropriately (such as the "I froze in my tracks" responses that sometimes occur).

Competency Validation
Insertion of Peripheral Intravenous Catheters

Name _____   Unit/Clinic _____

Classification _____   Employee ID# _____

Prior to Return Demonstration: Date and Learner Signature

1. Successfully complete the IV Class or   _____
   Self Learning Packet "Starting a
   Peripheral IV."

2. Read/Review the IV Starting Policy   _____
   in the Practice Manual (33.14.2) and
   review the steps to IV starting in the
   Springhouse Illustrated Manual of
   Nursing Practice, pp. 121-128.

Return Demonstration:

3. When you are ready to perform an IV start, notify a qualified mentor to observe your return
   demonstration of skill.

                                                  Date and Mentor Signature

   • Staff with previous experience in
     starting IV must have one observation   1. _____
     with a qualified mentor.

   • Staff with no previous experience
     starting IVs must have three observations   1. _____
     with a qualified mentor
                                                  2. _____

                                                  3. _____

**All Mentors: Please review the "Mentor Expectations" on the back of this form before
observing someone on this competency.**

*__Mentor Qualifications:__ Anyone who successfully completes the above competency for
Peripheral IV starting. If you do not have someone in your area qualified, contact the Float
Pool. All staff in the Float Pool have been trained and observed.*

Mentor Expectations:

◆ Use the IV starting Policy (33.14.2) in the Practice Manual or the guidelines for IV starting in the <u>Illustrated Manual of Nursing Practice</u> (pp.121-128) to assess the technique of the person you are observing.

◆ Maintain safety for the patient at all times...

- Watch the employee through each step of the procedure.

- Stop the demonstration of skill at any point when the patient is being placed at risk.   (i.e. if sterile technique is breached -- interrupt the procedure.)

◆ If the individual has successfully completed the IV start, sign and date the competency form. If not, encourage the individual to review the procedure and try the return demonstration again later.

*Thank you for helping us maintain
quality care for our patient.*

If you have any questions about IV starting or this competency, feel free to call Educational Services at ext. 5353.

Date _____

Name _____

SS# _____

Crosstraining Skills Assessment
for Patient Care Technicians
Medical and Surgical Units

SKILL	REQUIRED FOR COMPLETION
A. Foley Catheter Discontinuation • Follow Paraprofessional Skills Guideline	☐ Observation of Foley Discontinuation by a Nurse _____ <div align=center>Nurse Signature</div>
B. Collecting UA/UC from Indwelling Catheters • Follow Paraprofessional Skills Guideline	☐ Observation of Collecting UA/UC from Indwelling Catheters by a Nurse _____ <div align=center>Nurse Signature</div>
C. Hemovac/Jackson Pratt Drain Stripping • Follow Paraprofessional Skills Guideline	☐ Completed 7C Orientation ☐ Observation by Nurse or Skilled Paraprofessional _____ <div align=center>Nurse or Paraprofessional Signature</div>
D. Hemovac/Jackson Pratt Dressing Change • Follow Paraprofessional Skills Guideline	☐ Observation of Hemovac/Jackson Pratt Dressing Change by a Nurse _____ <div align=center>Nurse Signature</div>
E. NG Canister Set-up/Emptying	☐ Completed 7C Orientation ☐ Observation by Nurse or Skilled Paraprofessional _____ <div align=center>Nurse or Paraprofessional Signature</div>
F. Chest Tubes	☐ Skills Fair Attendance _____ <div align=center>Instructor Signature</div>
G. Trach's	☐ Skills Fair Attendance _____ <div align=center>Instructor Signature</div>

SKILL	REQUIRED FOR COMPLETION
H. Suprapubic Catheter Dressing Change • Follow Paraprofessional Skills Guideline	☐ Observation of Suprapubic Dressing Change by an nurse
	_____ Nurse Signature
I. Pnemoboots Application	☐ Self Review of at least one application
	_____ Observer's Signature

* A "skilled paraprofessional" is any Patient Care Technician or Nursing Assistant who has worked on the unit for 1 year or more.

Observation of Daily Work

Observation of daily work can measure skills in the technical domain.

Many of the skills we need to verify in individuals are demonstrated every day in the work setting. Using the actions we demonstrate on a daily basis to do our job is a valid form of competency assessment.

Here are some examples:

- **How can you verify that a secretary knows how to use a given software package on the computer?**

   Observation of daily practice = The secretary submits a document produced using that package (for example, the budget spread sheet, a newsletter, and so on).

- **We just got voice mail and e-mail in some departments. How do we verify the competency for something like that?**

   Observation of daily practice = Have each person send e-mail/voice mail messages to the others or to a central location.

- **We have staff who need to assemble equipment, food trays, sterile trays, and other items. How do I measure the competency for those tasks?**

   Observation of daily practice = Observe the finished product.

Sometimes observation of daily work is so obvious that we forget to use it as a verification method. Keep in mind that the observer of the finished product or action can be a supervisor or a peer. By using other team members, you promote team building.

Example:
In one hospital the ortho unit and med-surg units would call Physical Therapy to send someone to set up orthopedic trapeze equipment for patient beds. Physical therapy would

send a Physical Therapy Assistant (PTA) to set them up. This activity was often done without anyone observing (which is normal).

As a routine, before transferring a patient into a bed with this new set-up, nurses overseeing this transfer will check the stability and set-up of the trapeze unit. This hospital realized that it was already assessing competency through its daily routines. Now the hospital just needed to capture it.

The staff decided to change the equipment request tag on the trapeze equipment to capture this competency assessment. The request tag was placed on the equipment by materials services to track and charge the equipment to the right location and patient. On the new request tag they included a space for the signature of the person who set up the equipment on the patient bed. They also added a space for the nurse to sign when he or she double-checked the equipment set-up prior to placing the patient in the bed with this equipment. A question was asked in this space, "Was the set-up done accurately. If no, what was not correct?"

When the equipment was disassembled and sent back to materials services, the tags on the equipment were removed and sent back to Physical Therapy. The employees could then use this data to validate their competencies related to equipment set-up.

This is a great example of capturing the competency assessment activities already being done in our organizations on a daily basis. It also shows a great way for departments to support each other in developing more effective strategies for meaningful competency assessment.

Case Studies

Case studies are great for measuring critical thinking skills.

Case studies generally provide individuals with a situation and ask them to explain their responses or choices in that given situation.

Case studies can be prepared many different ways:

- Create a story of a patient or situation. Then ask questions that reflect that situation and capture the nature of the competency you are measuring. (Caution: This approach can sometimes lead the employee to the correct answer just by what is included or not included in the story.)

- Identify questions that capture the nature of the competency you are trying to measure, and have the employees use their real-life situations as the story. Then they can use the list of general questions identified to demonstrate their critical thinking skills in a real-life situation.

This second approach to case studies is much better at revealing application to real-world situations. It also helps assess the employees' ability to observe. As they explain the story or situation, they are showing their observation skills. The more they are able to consciously observe, the better their choice in the situation will be.

Case studies can be used alone or shared in discussion groups for further teambuilding and group problem-solving. (See the "discussion groups" section in this chapter for more examples of this verification method.)

Diabetes Case Study

Elizabeth is a 37 year old female with insulin dependent diabetes. She was admitted two days ago to the ICU with hyperglycemia and peripheral neuropathy. Blood glucose on admission was 970. She cannot remember when she last took her insulin. She was transferred from the ICU to the Med-Surg Unit today. Information on transfer at 2:00 pm includes:

- Blood sugar = 320
- Insulin pump discontinued 2 hours before transfer
- LOC = Oriented X 3
- Lower extremities test out slightly weak bilaterally

In the evening Elizabeth walks to her doorway and calls to the desk, "Did I leas the oven on? Can someone check? As you help her back to bed you note her speech is slow. She is also cool and clammy. Her gait is ataxic and she has difficulty getting into bed. Her coordination seems off.

What neurologic changes are happening to this patient?

Is this patient showing signs of hypoglycemia? If so, what are they?

What nursing actions would you continue or initiate during your shift with this patient?

Age Specific Aspect:
Would you consider anything different in your actions if this was a 87 year old woman rather than a 37 year old woman?

CRITICAL THINKING DOMAIN
Staffing Case Study

It is 5:30 Saturday morning, census is 381. There are requests for 39 float nurses and 12 paraprofessionals. All staff currently working are aware of how short staffing is and have already been asked to stay. In fact there are 17 staff people already doubling from the previous shift. Individual PCU's have called all their own staff, doubles and partial doubles have been confirmed and you still have 18 unmet requests for nurses. Some charge nurses have stated that if no more help is available patient care will not be safe. The staff/scheduler looks to you for assistance and direction.

I.   What factors do you assess?

II.   Remembering your timeline, prioritize your possible interventions and decisions.

III. How would you assess the effectiveness of your actions/decisions?

ETHICS CASE NO. 3 -

You are a Human Resources Assistant at your firm.

By virtue of your position, you are aware of the confidential information that, within the next three months, there will be a major "lay-off" of employees.

Your best friend is also an employee of your company. And, you have learned that she is on the list of employees to be relieved of their jobs.

Your friend is also in the process of purchasing a new home.

You are certain that, if your friend had any idea she would soon be losing her job, she would not even be contemplating the purchase of this larger, more expensive home.

If you tipped her off, you would obviously be saving her considerable anxiety later on.

What (if anything) would you do?

Pain Management Case Studies

Two patients are presented. For each patient you are asked to make decisions about pain and medication

Case Study A

Edward is 30 years old and has been hospitalized following a fractured hip sustained in a skiing accident two days ago. Your assessment yields the following information: no history of allergies of chronic illness; receiving vitamins and diet supplements; weight = 165; BP = 120/80; HR = 80; R = 18; on a scale of 0 to 5 (0 = no pain/discomfort, 5 = worst pain/discomfort), Edward rates his hip pain as 4.

1. On the patient's record you must mark his pain on the scale below. Circle the number that represents your assessment of Edward's pain:

   0   1   2   3   4   5

   No pain/discomfort   Worst pain/discomfort

2. Your assessment, above, is made four hours after Edward received morphine 10 mg. IM. During the 3 hours following the injection, Edward's pain ratings ranged from 3 to 4 and he had no clinically significant respiratory depression, sedation, or other untoward side effects. His physician's order for analgesia is "morphine IM 5 to 15 mg. q3-4h PRN pain relief." Check the action you will take at this time:

   ____a) Administer no morphine at this time.
   ____b) Administer morphine 5mg. IM now.
   ____c) Administer morphine 10mg. IM now.
   ____d) Administer morphine 15 mg. IM now.

3. Is your medication choice, above, determined by your concern that any of the following are likely to occur in this particular patient? Check all that apply.

   ____a) respiratory depression
   ____b) addiction (psychological dependence)
   ____c) tolerance to analgesia
   ____d) physical dependence (withdrawal)
   ____e) other; specify _____
   ____f) non of the above are major concerns

Case Study B

Frank is 75 years old and has been hospitalized following fractured hip sustained in a fall two daysago. Your assessment yields the following information: history of arthritis and hyper tension, receiving antihypertensive and anti-inflammatory medications; weight 150; BP = 150/90; HR = 80; R = 18; on a scale of 0 to 5 (0 = no pain/discomfort, 5 = worst pain/discomfort), Frank rates his hip pain as 4.

1. On the patient's record you must mark his pain on the scale below. Circle the number that represents your assessment of Frank's pain:

```
     0              1              2              3              4              5
No pain/discomfort                                                    Worst pain/discomfort
```

2. Your assessment, above, is made four hours after Frank received morphine 10 mg. IM. During the 3 hours following the injection, Frank's pain ratings changed from 3 to 4 and he had no clinically significant respiratory depression, sedation, or other untoward side effects. His physician's order for analgesia is "morphine IM 5 to 15 mg. q3-4h PRN pain relief." Check the action you will take at this time:

____a)   Administer no morphine at this time.
____b)   Administer morphine 5mg. IM now.
____c)   Administer morphine 10mg. IM now.
____d)   Administer morphine 15 mg. IM now.

3. Is your medication choice, above, determined by your concern that any of the following are likely to occur in this particular patient? Check all that apply.

____a) respiratory depression
____b) addiction (psychological dependence)
____c) tolerance to analgesia
____d) physical dependence (withdrawal)
____e) other; specify _____
____f) none of the above are major concerns

There is no one right answer to these case studies. However, it is important to examine why you selected the answers you did. Your answers reflect your beliefs and values. Take some time to review your answers based on the pain assessment algorithm and information below.

Reflection for Case Study A and B

The major difference between Edward and Frank are their ages. Managing an elder's pain can be challenging. Many people don't know the factors that can impede optimal pain management.

Elderly patients are often undertreated for cancer pain. Attitudes of health care professionals, the public, and patients toward pain can impede appropriate care; because many people consider acute and chronic pain to be a part of normal aging. In some instances, pain is not assessed because elderly patients, who may be confused, have difficulty communicating their pain to health professionals. In other instances, clinicians have mistaken beliefs about decreased pain sensitivity and heightened pain tolerance in the elderly. Frequently, the elderly are given nonopioids or weak doses of medications because their care providers mistakenly believe that they cannot tolerate opioid agents.

The elderly should be considered an at-risk group for the under treatment of cancer pain because of inappropriate beliefs about their pain sensitivity, pain tolerance, and ability to use opioids. Elderly patients, like other adults, require aggressive pain assessment and management.

Pain management in the elderly presents several challenges, including the discrepancy between the high prevalence of pain in the elderly and the limited attention to this group in the research literature and in medical and nursing texts (Ferrell, 1991). Of all reports about pain published annually, fewer than 1 percent focus on pain experience or syndromes in the elderly (Melding, 1991). Current pharmacologic research is often limited to single-dose studies in young or middle-aged adults and does not assess the complications and side effects of medications in the elderly. Elderly patients who participate in pain clinics or studies are likely to be the mobile elderly. Furthermore, elderly patients are often excluded from rehabilitation programs and aggressive treatment of pain (Middaugh, Levin, Kee, et al., 1988; Sorkin, Ruby, Hanlon, et al., 1990).

In spite of the lack of research, there is evidence that the elderly experience more pain than younger people. It has been estimated that the prevalence of pain in those older than 60 years of age (250 per 1,000) is double that in those younger than 60 (125 per 1,000) (Crook, Rideout, and Browne, 1984). Among the institutionalized elderly, the prevalence of pain may be over 70 percent (Ferrell, Ferrell, and Osterweil, 1990). Elderly patients with cancer often have other chronic diseases, more than one source of pain, and complex medication regimens that place them at increased risk for drug-drug as well as drug-disease interactions.

Cognitive impairment, delirium (common among the acutely ill elderly), and dementia (which occurs in as many as 50 percent of the institutionalized elderly) pose serious barriers to pain assessment (Kane, Oulander, and Abrass, 1989) Psychometric properties of pain assessment instruments, such as VAS, verbal descriptor, and numerical scales, have not been established in this population. Moreover, a high prevalence of visual, hearing, and motor impairments in the elderly impede the use of these tools. Research on the nursing home population shows that many patients with mild to moderate cognitive impairment are able to report pain reliably at the moment or when prompted, although their pain recall may be less reliable. **These findings suggest that this population may require more frequent pain assessment than patients who are not cognitively impaired.** (Ferrell, in press).

Nonopioid analgesics, including acetaminophen and other NSAIDs, are helpful adjuncts to opioids for cancer-related pain. The risk for gastric and renal toxicity from NSAIDs is increased among elderly patients, however, and unusual drug reactions including cognitive impairment, constipation, and headache are also more common (Roth, 1989). Factors that may contribute to altered side effects in the elderly include multiple medical diagnoses, multiple drug interactions, and altered pharmacokinetics. If gastric ulceration is a concern, NSAIDs with lower gastric toxicity (e.g., choline magnesium trisalicylate) should be chosen. The coadministration of misoprostol should also be considered as a way to protect the gastric mucosa.

Opioids are effective for the management of cancer pain in most elderly patients. In the elderly, Cheyne-Stokes respiratory patterns are not unusual during sleep and need not prompt the discontinuation of opioid analgesia. Elderly people tend to be more sensitive to the analgesic effects of opioids, experiencing high peak effect and longer duration of pain relief (Kaiko, 1980). The elderly, especially those who are opioid naive, also tend to be more sensitive to sedation and respiratory depression, probably as a result of alterations in metabolism and in the distribution and excretion of the drugs. For this reason, the prolonged use of longer acting drugs such as methadone requires caution (Ferrell, 1991).

Elderly people in general have increased fat-to-lean body mass ratios and reduced glomerular filtration rates. Opioids produce cognitive and neuropsychiatric dysfunction through poorly defined mechanism that in part include the accumulation of biologically active metabolites such as morphine-6-glucuronide or normeperidine (Melzack, 1990). Opioid dosage titration should take into account not only analgesic effects but also side effects that extend beyond cognitive impairment. Such side effects may include urinary retention (a threat in elderly males with prostatic hyperplasia), constipation and intestinal obstruction, or respiratory depression.

Local anesthetic infusions, including lidocaine or opioids, may result in cognitive impairment if significant drug levels in the blood are reached. Orthostatic hypotension and clumsiness may result from tricyclic antidepressant administration and other medications used for pain management and concurrent medical illnesses. Precautions, such as assistance during ambulation, should be taken to prevent falls and fractures.

PCA was shown to be safe and effective for postoperative pain relief among elderly patients (Egbert, Parks, Short, et al., 1990). PCA has not been extensively studied for long-term use in the elderly with cancer-related pain. The use of any "high-tech" pain treatment such as PCA or intraspinal analgesia should be titrated and monitored especially closely because of the elderly patient's increased sensitivity to drug effects (Ferrell, Cronin Nash, and Warfield, 1992).

"Learning on the Fly" Case Studies

Case Study #1

You are the manager for a group of 40 people. You are preparing to have a performance review with one of the employees you supervise. You see them in the hall the day before the review and confirm the time you are meeting. They agree, and briefly mention they would like to discuss possible leave options based on the new parental leave laws. As you return to your office you realize you have not a clue what the law says or how the organization has responded to these legal parameters. You need to figure this out before your meeting tomorrow at 11:00 am, so you can at least discuss it with some knowledge. This will mean "Learning on the Fly."

What are some of the things you would do to educate yourself?

What are some of your resources for this type of issue?

What would you do if the employee asked you questions you could not answer?

Submit this case study along with your competency record to your supervisor as indicated.

"Learning on the Fly" Case Studies

Case Study #2

You are leading a committee that has been asked to implement a new automated machine to do the work more efficiently in your area. Your committee members were selected to implement this project because of their knowledge of the service area. No one on the committee has every implemented a project of this nature, and this will be your first try at something like this as well. So your group is familiar with the service needs but not knowledgeable of how to go about implementing a change of this nature.

As the leader of this committee, where would you begin in preparing this group to carry out its assignment?

What would you do to prepare yourself for leading this group?

What resources would you rely on if your group ran into roadblocks along the way?

Submit this case study along with your competency record to your supervisor as indicated

Charge Nurse Staffing Skills Competency (ICU)

This is one method to meet the Charge Nurse competency. Any unit or individual may develop a method of assessment as long is it meets the criteria for the competency and is approved by your unit education council.

To Complete the Charge Nurse Skill Worksheet

- Familiarize yourself with the staffing policies attached.

- Use the worksheet to make staffing assignments for the unit illustrated.

Tips

◆ Don't make it more complex than it is. Only use information given, even if it is sketchy.

◆ In this scenario we have not included the use of paraprofessionals or assigning patients to the CN. This is just an exercise in matching staff to patient needs.

Charge Nurse Skill Worksheet
(ICU)

You are the charge nurse on this ICU. You have 5 patients and 4 staff listed below. Please use the criteria in the staff policies attached and the information below to make your staffing assignments.

Room 3
46 y/o female with ARDS & vent dependent, active weaning-stable

door

Room 4
Fresh post-CABG pt to arrive ~ 1pm

window

window

Room 2
68 y/o man post MI, on IABP (balloon pump)-drips but no titrating at this time

door

Room 1
Post PTCA pt-stable, will have femoral sheaths pulled and be txd out later this morning

PCU
Desk
Area

Room 5
35 y/o Hmong man with active TB, vented, strict isolation

Nurses

Indicate Room(s) assigned to each nurse.

Jeff
  • ICU nurse from the float pool
  • Has floated to your unit 3 times
  • Fully oriented

Jane
  • Unit staff nurse for 4 yrs
  • IABP certified

Barb
  • Unit staff nurse for 3 yrs
  • Pregnant

Ann
  • Med-Surg nurse floating from med-surg unit
  • No ICU training

_____ has successfully demonstrated the appropriate use of staff criteria to match patient care requirements with nursing personnel skill levels.

_____   _____
    Date   Competency Reviewer

TITLE: **STAFFING ASSIGNMENTS**		MANUAL Policy Manual
AUTHOR:	POSITION:	FILE ALPHABETICALLY IN SECTION:
APPROVAL BODY:	CHAIR:	REVIEW DATE:
		REVISION DATE:

POLICY

The Charge Nurse or Nurse Manager is responsible for patient assignment
of staff. The following criteria are considered in determining staffing
assignments for each shift:

a) Experience and expertise of available staff
   1) Educational preparation
   2) Qualifications of staff
   3) Orientation completed
   4) Role limitations (including clinical practice limitations of Float Pool
      staff, see Nursing Services policy)
b) Patient classification data
c) Patient care needs/priorities, including patient teaching and discharge
   planning needs
d) PCU care delivery system
e) Infection control parameters
f) Health status or limitations of staff
g) Special interests of staff
h) Availability of support/specialist resources
i) Patient requests
j) Geography of PCU

To the extent possible, an RN will make a patient assessment before
delegating appropriate aspects of nursing care to ancillary personnel.

Nursing Services staff will be assigned accountability to all patients, even when
nursing students are given primary assignment.

REVIEWING AUTHORITY	TITLE	DATE

06334, JUL 90

> Other policies that may be helpful in making staffing assignments.

According to policy 33.15 (Infection Control) found in the hospital policy manual:

A pregnant nurse should not be assigned a patient who has the following infectious diseases:
>> Rubella
>> VZV
>> Measles
>> Mumps

Pregnant nurses can be assigned to patients who have:
>> CMV
>> HIV
>> HBV (Hepatitis B)

According to policy "Chemotherapy Administration" found in the Medication Manual:

- Nurses must complete chemo orientation before giving chemo.

- Only RNs on the PCU can administer chemo (nurses floating to the unit can give oral chemo and monitor continuous infusions initiated by an RN on the PCU).

- Pregnant nurses may be assigned to chemo patients. They are at no greater risk than a non-pregnant nurse if proper technique is used.

Other ICU information:

- Patients in the ICU should be visualized at all times - either physically or by EKG monitor.

- Only ICU nurses who have taken and passed the balloon pump exam can care for patients on IABP.

- Nurses floating to the ICU who have no ICU training should be buddied with another ICU nurse, rather than having their own assignment.

Charge Nurse Staffing Skills Competency
ICU Answers

Jane must have Room 2 since she is the only nurse scheduled who is certified to take care of patients on an intra-aortic balloon pump.

Ann should be buddied with a nurse having a paired assignment because, having no ICU training, she shouldn't probably have her own patient assignment.

Room 4 should not be a single assignment to a nurse because the patient isn't arriving until 1pm and the assigned nurse would have no other patients until then.

Jeff and Barb can have any assignments except Room 2.

Exemplars

Exemplars can be used to measure critical thinking skills, as well as interpersonal skills.

An exemplar is a story you tell or write yourself. It describes a situation you have experienced, or describes rationale you thought about and choices you made in a situation.

Exemplars can assess not only critical thinking and interpersonal skills but also many skills that are impossible to observe. Exemplars are one of the few verification methods that can capture actions that are not taken—especially when "not taking action" is the competency choice in a given situation.

Example:

A venipuncture technician comes to draw blood from a patient. The technician finds the patient crying, and there are several family member in the patient's room. They seem to be discussing some sensitive issues. The venipuncture technician chooses to skip this blood draw and go to the others in the area. When the technician checks back later, the patient is still talking with family members. The venipuncture technician checks the chart for information on the nature of the draw, and discusses with the nurse the possibility of deferring the draw until later.

Very little of this competent action on the part of the venipuncture technician can be observed. But if the employee describes this situation in an exemplar story, you could easily see the critical thinking process used. You could also tell the difference between this situation and one in which an employee is trying to avoid doing his or her job. The rationale for the choices made would be as clear as in the situation above.

Exemplars can be used for any job class. They are great for both staff and leadership positions. They are especially great for job classes that require establishing trust with a client, providing customer service, or dealing with sensitive issues.

Primary Nursing Exemplar

This form can be used as a personal exemplar (case study reflecting your performance)
or can be used by another individual to provide you with peer review.

Name _____   Unit/Clinic/Area _____

Job Title _____   Date _____

This form reflects my contribution to our primary nursing model through the following
competency statement: (select the one that best describes you role)

❑ Primary Nurse -- demonstrates accountability to care delivery through planning
and coordinating

❑ Associate Nurses, Paraprofessional caregivers, and Clinical Specialists
demonstrates support to primary nursing model through communication and
actions supporting the achievement of patient care outcomes

❑ Leadership, Management, Educators -- demonstrates accountability to primary
nursing model by facilitation of activities that support this practice.

Describe one for more situation that demonstrates your accountability to the Primary Nursing
Care Delivery Model. Your description should include one or all of the components of primary
nursing listed below:

Primary Nursing is carried out when:

◆ the nurse-patient relationship engenders trust, and provides consistency and advocacy.

◆ continuity of care is provided.

◆ there is coordinated and efficient planning for transitions to other sites of care.

◆ there is an explicit plan of care focused on meeting identified outcomes.

◆ effective communication within the health care team occurs.

◆ the patient and family are involved in the planning, implementation, and evaluation of care.

(over)

Use this space to describe a situation that demonstrates your contribution to our primary nursing model: (Check out the samples on the next page to help get you started.)

Completed by:

❑ Self   _____
                                    Signature

❑ Peer   _____
                                    Signature

Submit this form with your competency record to your department supervisor.

Some samples to get you started:

Last week I was caring for Mrs. F, a rehab patient.
In the Kardex I read the care plan written by the
primary nurse. It said we need to increase her
fluid intake over the next few days. As the NA,
I have been assisting Mrs. F. with her meals. She
has a tough time holding a glass. She does better
with a mug. She can even pick up a mug by
herself. I have been setting up a mug full of
water or juice every 2 hours for Mrs. F. This
encourages her to drink a little all day. I
also wrote that she handles a mug better
than a glass in the Kardex for the primary
nurse and other care givers.

Mary Lipton, NA

I decided to be the primary nurse for Mr. C.
after I took care of him after surgery. I found
out his wife had just passed away only three
months before, and I had a feeling he would
not be able to return home on his own. The
first day after surgery I called the social
worker to make them aware of Mr C's need
for transitional care or possibly home care.
I met Mr. C's son the 2nd day post-op. He was
very happy I was exploring ways to provide help
after discharge. With his mother's sudden death,
he was concerned about his father's care at home
I arranged a meeting with the son, SW, MD, &
myself. I know the doctors were planning to
discharge him soon and there was alot of
planning to do. I also asked the associate
nurses for their input. We concluded that
Mr. C. should go home with visits from a
home health aide.

Sally Adams, RN

Customer Service Exemplar

An exemplar is a story you tell or write about what you did. Please share your story about how you supported our customer service principles this year. Your customer may be the patient, family, visitors, or a fellow employees. It will vary depending on where you work.

Our customer service principles include:

- Treating the customer with kindness and respect
- Calling the customer by name, and showing genuine interest
- Listening to what the customer has to say
- Helping the customer get the help they need -- Avoid saying, "That's not my job." Instead say, "Let's find someone who can help you."

Share your story in this space. It does not have to be long. Examples of other stories are found on the back of this form.

Your name _____ Date _____

Dept./Work area _____ Job Title _____

Please submit this form with your competency assessment record to your supervisor.

Customer Service Exemplar written by a social worker
(The patient is the customer)

I was visiting a patient the other day in their hospital room. During our visit, the patient said they needed help getting up to the bathroom. I told the patient, "I'm not sure about your restrictions, or the best way to help you, so I am going to quick check with the nursing staff. I will be back in two minutes. I smiled and went to find some help. I found the charge nurse, and asked for help. Together we went back to the room and look at the chart to see the patient needed at least one person to walk with her, and her urine needed to be measured. I helped walk her to the bathroom and the charge nurse set up the urine collector in the toilet.

Customer Service Exemplar written by a volunteer
(A visitor is the customer)

I was on my way to lunch when a visitor stopped me in the hallway and said, "Where is the cholesterol screening being done today?" Well, I had no idea where it was, but I said to the visitor, "I'm not sure, but let me take you to the information desk. They can probably help us find out where it is today.

Customer Service Exemplar written by a computer support person
(A fellow employee is the customer)

I got a call from Sarah, a nurse manager, who just hired a new employee and needed to get him into computer training. I asked Sarah if this was the first employee she had sent to computer training, and she said yes. Then I said, "I will E-mail you the steps you need to do to assign a computer ID and get the employee into training. If you have any questions, Sarah, just give me a call or send me an E-mail. I'm here to help."

Building Bridges Exemplar

We need to break down the walls between groups and department ... and begin to build bridges.

Through patient surveys and observation of our daily work at Mercy/Unity, it is evident that we have built a few wall between groups. Some people have described us as a group of silos. We are all working hard in our areas, but not communicating or collaborating as well as we should with other groups and departments.
We need to make an effort to change this.
We need to start building bridges

Take some time and energy this year to build a bridge somewhere. Here are some ways you can achieve this:

◆ Get to know someone in another department. This can be done in person or over the phone. The next time you talk with them regarding your daily business, call them by name, ask them how their day is going, and thank them for their support.

◆ Include other groups in committee or group work. Think of other groups or departments that may benefit from the work issues to be addressed. Don't just tell them about it "after the fact." Include them from the beginning.

◆ The way we communicate can keep many walls between us. Watch for statements like, *"that's their problem."* Instead we should ask, *"how can I support you as you address this problem."*

No matter where we work or what our role is at Mercy/Unity, we all need to have the skills and the willingness to help build bridges. Please describe below one situation this year where you made an effort to build a bridge.

Name _____   Date _____

Submit this form with your competency record.

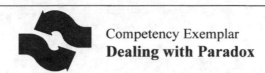

Competency Exemplar
Dealing with Paradox

A paradox is something that seems to be contradictory. Leaders often deal with paradox everyday. Finding a balance in the paradox is key to successful leadership.

- Being tough and compassionate
- Being empathic and objective
- Being able to lead and follow
- Being an individual contributor and a team player
- Being self confident and appropriately humble
- Finding agreement in conflict

All of these require a leader to see the larger purpose and exercise critical thinking skills. To demonstrate your efforts in "Dealing with Paradox," share a situation where you found yourself in a paradox.

•Briefly share your paradoxical situation

•Explain if you would do anything different if that situation occurred again.

Completed by _____ Date _____

Submit this exemplar with your competency record to your supervisor as indicated.

Competency Exemplar
Learning on the Fly

Learning is a lifelong process.
We need to become comfortable with learning as we go.
Take some time to reflect on your skills of learning.

Learning on the fly requires us to…

• Learn quickly when we are faced with new problems and challenges
• Be open to change
• Analyze both successes and failures for clues to improve
• Try new solutions to problems
• Enjoy the challenges of unfamiliar tasks
• Search for the underlying structure and essence of the situations we encounter.

Please share an experience you have had this past year that demonstrated one or all of these concepts required to "Learn on the Fly."

Completed by _____   Date _____

Submit this exemplar with your competency record to your supervisor as indicated.

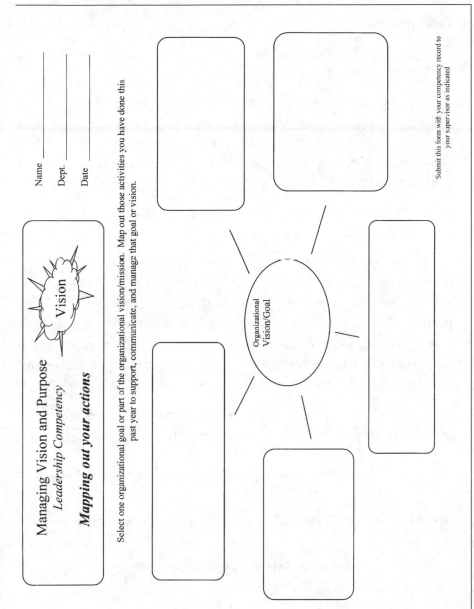

Name _____

Dept. _____

Date _____

Managing Vision and Purpose
Leadership Competency

Mapping out your actions

Select one organizational goal or part of the organizational vision/mission. Map out those activities you have done this past year to support, communicate, and manage that goal or vision.

Vision

Organizational
Vision/Goal

Submit this form with your competency record to
your supervisor as indicated

Peer review

Peer review can be used to measure interpersonal skills, as well as critical thinking skills.

Peer review is a very powerful tool to help reinforce the behaviors we would like to see in our teams. Peer review can be a positive, motivating experience or it can be a devestatingly negative experience. It all depends how it is approached and carried out.

Here are a few tips to help you create successful, respectful peer review.

There are two types of peer reviews: written and face-to-face. Both can provide a great deal of support and encouragement to an employee if carried out in a respectful, very planned-out way. If you have never done peer review, start with written peer review. Face-to-face peer review can be very threatening, especially if you have never experienced success with the peer review process in the past.

To create a healthy approach to whichever peer review approach you take, keep these three aspects in mind.

- Make the process safe for the person **receiving** the information.
- Make the process safe for the person **giving** the information.
- Make it safe for the person **facilitating** the process.

Communication Assessment Peer Survey

Many skills are required to successfully carry out any job. Communication is one of those skills. This survey is designed to provide feedback to employees on their communication skills.

(See some of our communication goals on the back)

Employee's name _____

Dept./Work area _____   Job Title _____

When I am talking with this employee:

	Agree				Disagree
1. I feel he/she is listening to what I say	1	2	3	4	5
2. I feel he/she speaks honestly and directly to me	1	2	3	4	5
3. I feel this individual makes an effort to clarify differences.	1	2	3	4	5

Comments:

Your name _____   Date _____

Dept. _____   Job Title _____

Helpful hints in assessing communication competency and support growth of healthy responses:

◆ Speak for yourself, and use "I" statements whenever possible.

    Example: "I feel left out when you don't communication the updates you have." That's much better than... "You never tell us what is going on!"

◆ Listening respectfully involves clarify and reassuring the person that you have heard them.

    Example: "So you are saying that you feel...."

◆ Listening respectfully, does not mean that you agree with the individual. It only means you understand what they are saying to you.

Communication is an art.
There can be lots of different interpretations to one event.
Successful communication focuses on respecting ourselves and each other regardless of the opinions we may hold.

Dealing with Ambiguity
Leadership Competency Assessment
Peer Review

As a fellow colleague, I value your opinion of my performance. Please take some time to share your thoughts. When you are done please send it to _____
by _____.
　　　　　　　　　Date

Employee Name _____　　　Peer Completing Form _____

Dept./Title _____　　　Dept./Title _____

　　　　　　　　　　　　　　　　　　Date _____

Through your observation and interactions with the employee above, please answer the following questions. This information will be compiled with others to assist the employee and supervisor in reinforcing and improving skills related to dealing with ambiguity.

This individual...	Agree				Disagree
1. Can effectively cope with change.	1	2	3	4	5
2. Can shift gears comfortably.	1	2	3	4	5
3. Can decide and act without having the total picture.	1	2	3	4	5
4. Isn't upset when things are up in the air.	1	2	3	4	5
5. Doesn't have to finish things before moving on.	1	2	3	4	5
6. Can comfortably handle risk and uncertainty.	1	2	3	4	5

Comments:

Thanks for your feedback.

Customer Service
Peer Review

Please briefly describe the customer service you observed or received from your fellow coworker.

Our customer service principles include:

- Treating the customer with kindness and respect
- Calling the customer by name, and showing genuine interest
- Listening to what the customer has to say
- Helping the customer get the help they need -- Avoid saying, "That's not my job." Instead say, "Let's find someone who can help you."

Employee's name _____

Dept./Work area _____   Job Title _____

Briefly describe how this employee contributed to good customer service:

Your name _____   Date _____

Dept. _____   Job Title _____

Coping with and Managing Change

Peer Review Worksheet

This form may be used to verify your competency related to "coping and managing change." Managing change is a skill that we will all need to survive the changes occurring in health care today. Give this form to a peer and ask them for feedback related to your skills in coping and managing change.

	Never	Rarely	Sometimes	Frequently	Always
1. When confronted with a new idea, this individual reflects on the idea before responding.	1	2	3	4	5
2. When a system or issue needs changing this person is comfortable collecting information about the problem and possible solutions.	1	2	3	4	5
3. Most of the time this individual appears to have energy to cope with the fast-paced change occurring around me.	1	2	3	4	5
4. This person accepts responsibility for their personal response to the changes around them.	1	2	3	4	5
5. This person accepts accountability to educate themselves in becoming more comfortable with the change process.	1	2	3	4	5
6. This individual accepts responsibility for how to share their discomfort with the difficult parts of change. i.e. knowing when and where to appropriately share or discuss issues	1	2	3	4	5

Total = _____

Person being reviewed _____   Peer completing the review _____

To the individual being assessed:

Total up the numbers you circled for each statement. If your total is between 21 - 30, you are doing great. Keep up the good work. If your total is between 11 and 20, you have made a great start keep it up. If your total is between 0 and 10, we appreciate your honesty, and encourage you to participate in one of the "Managing Change" activities offered throughout the year.

Contact

[   ]

for more information

Submit this form with your competency assessment record.

FORM
Coping with and
Managing Change
Peer Review

FORM
Cardiopulmonary
Services
Peer Review

Cardiopulmonary Services

Health Team Member Review

Cardiopulmonary Services Practitioner: _____

1) How does this coworker maintain a professional attitude in interactions with patients and healthcare workers?

2) How are you aware that this coworker understands the technical and theoretical aspects of Respiratory Care including respiratory anatomy and physiology, respiratory care equipment, respiratory pharmacology, etc.?

3) How does this coworker provide an atmosphere of trust, respect, and effective communication towards patients and their families?

4) How does this coworker show responsibility of effective planning and organization? Are appropriate resources utilized to solve problems?

5) How does this coworker strive for effective communication and good relationships with other members of the healthcare team?

INTERPERSONAL DOMAIN
COMMUNICATION

To the Reviewer: As a part of my competency assessment, I am asking you to review my skills in the following areas. Please use the scale for each item; space is provided for any comments you make wish to make. Your feedback is greatly appreciated!

Rating scale: 1   2   3   4   5

                    Poor   Excellent

A. Provides peer/colleague with accurate information in a timely manner.

B. Direct (face-to-face) interactions with peer/colleague reflect skills of:

     1. listening respectfully

     2. giving feedback directly and honestly

     3. talking with others to clarify differences

C. Nondirect (telephone, etc.) interactions with colleagues reflect skills of:

     1. listening carefully

     2. giving feedback directly and honestly

     3. talking with others to clarify differences

Partners in Practice
Competencies for Success

Successful partnerships in care delivery require the following elements:

◆ Partnerships that use open and honest communication

◆ Support from leaders and non-partnered staff

◆ Recognition of the unique skills we all bring to partners regardless of job title or levels of educational preparation.

As part of the team carrying out "Partners in Practice," we need to each demonstrate our ability to contribute to quality care through partnerships.

Each member of the unit must complete the following Partners in Practice Competency by _____.

Competency statement	Verification Method (select one)	Date Completed
Actively participate in the promotion and implementation of Partnerships for successful care delivery.	❑ Have two peers complete the Partners in Practice Competency Peer Review ❑ Participant in one of the Partners in Practice Competency Discussion Groups (See _____ for dates and times)	

Partners in Practice Competency

Peer Review

Name _____

Unit/Clinic/Area _____   Job Title _____

Peer completing form _____

Unit/Clinic/Area _____   Job Title _____

This peer review reflects this person's ability to: *(select the one the fit the individual's job expectations)*

    ❑ Participate as a partner in a partnership

    ❑ Support partnership (even though they are not in a partnership that shift)

    ❑ Support partnerships through leadership, education, and/or communication

Please describe on the next page how this person supported and/or hindered the following ideas behind partnership:

◆ Uses open, honest communication (not engaging in backbiting, bickering, or blaming)

◆ Recognizing and using the unique talents of team member regardless of job title or educational preparation

◆ Supporting and contributing to partnership whether they are in the partnership or not.

◆ Sharing the work rather than focusing on dividing it equally.

◆ Celebrating our successes in delivering patient care together.

Thanks for taking the time to provide feedback
to help us achieve our care delivery goals.

Please return this completed peer review to _____ by _____

Self Assessment

Self assessment can measure critical thinking skills, especially values and beliefs.

Self Assessment is a verification method that is often avoided or used exclusively. Some people feel it is not a valid form of verification, so they do not use it at all. Other organizations tend to use it to verify all skills during orientation—asking the learners to check off when they feel they have achieved the skill. Neither of these approaches really applies this verification method in the way that best fits its purpose.

Self assessment is a valid form of competency assessment when applied to the appropriate competencies. Self assessment, like any other verification method, should not be used exclusively for all competencies. Self assessment is best used to assess aspects of the affective domain of learning. The affective domain includes those things such as values, beliefs, opinions, and attitudes. Self assessment engages the individual in a reflective exercise that allows him or her to explore some of the thoughts that influence day-to-day judgments. Just completing this form of verification has merit. It allows employees to reflect on and put into words their conscious and unconscious thoughts.

A self assessment verification tool should provide guidance to assist individuals in understanding the purpose of the verification tool and how to complete it. Not only can some self assessment tools help individuals judge their own competency level, but those tools can guide the individual to the appropriate actions to meet the required competency outcome level.

Self assessment has its place. Do not overuse it, but also do not avoid it. Self assessment can be a very valuable verification method for selected competencies.

FORM
Coping with and
Managing Change
Self Assessment
Worksheet

Coping with and Managing Change

Self Assessment Worksheet

This form may be used to verify your competency related to "coping and managing change." Managing change is a skill that we will all need to survive the changes occurring in health care today. Take sometime to reflect on the skills you will need to deal with change.

	Never	Rarely	Sometimes	Frequently	Always
1. When I am confronted with a new idea, I reflect on the idea before responding.	1	2	3	4	5
2. When a system or issue needs changing I feel comfortable collecting information about the problem and possible solutions.	1	2	3	4	5
3. Most of the time I feel I have enough energy to cope with the fast-paced change occurring around me.	1	2	3	4	5
4. I accept responsibility for my personal response to the changes around me.	1	2	3	4	5
5. I accept accountability to educate myself in becoming more comfortable with the change process.	1	2	3	4	5
6. I accept responsibility for how I share my discomfort with the difficult parts of change. i.e. knowing when and where to appropriately share or discuss issues	1	2	3	4	5

Total = _____

Total up the numbers you circled for each statement. If your total is between 21 - 30, you are doing great. Keep up the good work. If your total is between 11 and 20, you have made a great start keep it up. If your total is between 0 and 10, we appreciate your honesty, and encourage you to participate in one of the "Managing Change" activities offered throughout the year.

Contact

_____

for more information

Name _____   Date _____

Submit this form with your competency assessment record.

Pain Management Self Assessment Worksheet

The ABCDE process is the recommended clinical approach to pain management from the AHCPR Standards. Take some time to review your pain management practices with this process. Answer the following questions based on a patient you are caring for or have cared for in the past. Assess your own competency regarding pain management by comparing your patient assessment considerations with those on the algorithm attached to this page. This is also a great discussion group tool.

		Questions to Ask	Reflect on your patient care
A	Ask and Assess	• How often did you ask about their pain? • Did you assess pain systematically? e.g. Did you use a hierarchy of assessment techniques? • What intervals did you find suitable to assess pain after the intervention? e.g. 15-30 mins. after IV drug or 30 mins after oral drug or hours after non-drug interventions • Did you assess the patient with each NEW report of pain?	
B	Believe the patient.	• Did you believe the patient's self-report of pain? • How did you convey your belief of the patient regarding pain and experiences affecting their pain?	

Submit this form with your competency record

C	Choose appropriate interventions.	• How have you used different pain control options that are appropriate for this patient in this particular setting?
D	Deliver interventions.	• How have you delivered/coordinated interventions to reflect a timely, logical, coordinated approach to pain management?
E	Empower patients and families.	• How have you enabled patients to control their course of pain management as much as possible?

Algorithm of Pain Assessment Techniques

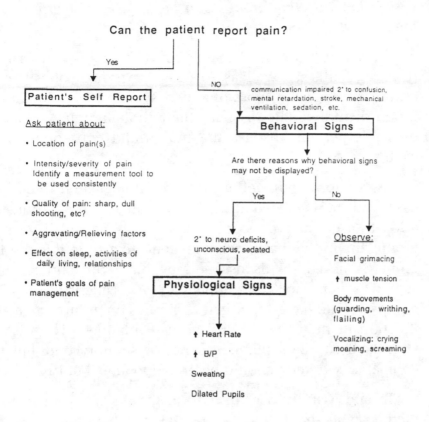

Can the patient report pain?

Yes

Patient's Self Report

NO — communication impaired 2˚ to confusion, mental retardation, stroke, mechanical ventilation, sedation, etc.

Ask patient about:

- Location of pain(s)

- Intensity/severity of pain
  Identify a measurement tool to
  be used consistently

- Quality of pain: sharp, dull
  shooting, etc?

- Aggravating/Relieving factors

- Effect on sleep, activities of
  daily living, relationships

- Patient's goals of pain
  management

Behavioral Signs

Are there reasons why behavioral signs
may not be displayed?

Yes   No

2˚ to neuro deficits,   Observe:
unconscious, sedated
                             Facial grimacing

Physiological Signs   ↑ muscle tension

                             Body movements
                             (guarding, writhing,
                             flailing)

↑ Heart Rate   Vocalizing: crying
                             moaning, screaming
↑ B/P

Sweating

Dilated Pupils

Warning: Discrepancies may occur between the three realms of assessment data. These discrepancies may result from several factors, including physiological adaptation to pain, coping skills acquired by patient, social/cultural expectations of behavior. **"The single most reliable indicator of the existence and intensity of acute pain -is the patient's self-report."** (AHCPR, Clinical Practice Guidelines, 92-0032, 11.)

Discussion/Reflection Groups

Discussion/reflection groups can be used to measure any of the three skill domains.

Discussion groups are a valid way to look at critical thinking skills, as well as to promote group cohesiveness and support. The purpose of a discussion group is to allow a group of individuals to share their thoughts and strategies on an issue, and discuss the merits and consequences of each aspect.

Discussion groups often use the strategies outlined in a case study, but go beyond the individual analysis of the situation to a group process of problem solving. In discussion groups the individual is asked to analyze a situation and the group is asked to discuss and evaluate the choices presented. When used for competency assessment, discussion groups should have a facilitator. Discussion groups are a verification method that should be well planned. The discussion itself can be a planned event or spontaneous, but the competency criteria should be prepared ahead of time.

To successfully use discussion groups as a verification method, you should have a facilitator. A facilitator is someone in the group who takes responsibility for overseeing the discussion and guiding the process. The facilitator should articulate the expectations of the competency and the use of discussion groups as a verification method. Also the form of evaluation should be described and discussed. Discussion groups are a purposeful event and the participants need to be aware of this.

Measuring critical thinking skills many not be familiar to or easy for many group facilitators. Here are a few strategies to help assess critical thinking competencies using discussion groups:

- Use a facilitator to guide the group through the process.
- Select a case study that has meaning to the group. See the section on case studies for some examples. You may also have the group bring a situation they have recently

encountered (for example, dealing with a difficult customer or situation).

- Identify some questions you will ask about the situation based on your organization's goals and philosophies.

- Competency assessment may be done by one individual or the group as a whole. Using the group to assess each participant's critical thinking skills builds a context for that behavior to continue outside the group. It is important to prepare the group to do this. Include some activities on giving and receiving feedback in a healthy, respectful way.

  - Establish expectations of the discussion group prior to the activity.

  - Each individual is responsible for any preparation needed prior to the discussion (read and answer case study questions).

  - Participants will contribute in the group discussion by sharing their ideas and discussing the merits and consequences of their responses and the responses of others.

  - Each individual will commit to providing a respectful environment for group discussion and support the group as a whole.

  - Each individual will look for ways to support his or her colleagues in the process.

  - Encourage the group to establish action plans for ongoing group support strategies and growth opportunities.

- Evaluation can be done by the group, if they have been prepared and educated to do this. The art of peer evaluation does take some time to develop, but is well worth the investment. If the group is unable to do this evaluation, or has difficulty carrying it out in some situations, the facilitator must be prepared to function as evaluator. Select facilitators that can assume this role if needed.

These simple strategies can help create a successful verification activity for critical thinking competencies. It can enhance group dynamics and promote ongoing communication among team members. Critical thinking competencies have always been difficult to capture. Discussion groups are one strategy to address this competency need.

Communication Assessment
Case Study/Discussion Group Tool

This competency tool can be used alone as a case study ***or***
as a case study to facilitate group discussion.
Groups discussions allows for a supportive way to assess competency regarding communication skills. Allowing peers to discuss
and give feedback to each other on potential responses helps assess skills and support growth of new skills in communication.

Describe a situation involving communication that has occurred recently that caused you to feel uneasy or
frustrated.

If you were in this situation...

How could you show to the individual(s) in this situation that you were listening to them?

In what way could you provide direct, honest, and respectful feedback or communication?

Describe some ways you could respectfully clarify differences or show disagreement?

Submit this form along with your competency record to your supervisor.

FORM
Partners in
Practice
Discussion Group
Activity

Partners in Practice Competency

Discussion Group Activity

Instructions:

1) Attend one of the discussion group sessions to discuss the following topics related to partnership and care deliver.

2) Share with the group your observations and experiences related to your recent partnership experiences and ways you can help improve or support the desired outcomes.

As you begin the discussion, keep in mind...

* *We will support the commitment card philosophies as we discussion thoughts.*

* *We do not have to agree with each other.*

* *We will look for ways to strengthen our relationships*

* *The discussion will focus on our relationships and professional behavior, and not on the division of tasks and assignments.*

• •

Questions to be discussed in the group:

What things helped us to "share the work" in a partnership?

What were some of the barriers to supporting the partnership concept?

What is something I can do differently that would help support or improve our partnership care delivery strategies?

What are some ways I can show support to my coworkers?

• •

Facilitators Guide to Discussion Group Competency Activity

1) Set up several discussion group times to discussion with staff the situations they recently encountered during care delivering using the partner model.

2) Begin the session by reviewing the purpose for the discussion group and the relationship guidelines you will use in the discussion (i.e. go over the Commitment to my Coworker card)

3) Create an environment that is safe and welcoming for all participants.

4) Review criteria for competency assessment below.
First and foremost, this is not a test with RIGHT answers. The goal is to create discussion and address ways to improve our relationships and support quality care deliver.

Measurement for individual competency:

-- Everyone must participate and share something to complete this competency activity.

-- The discussion must include each person articulating a way they will support the partnership model and its ongoing improvement. So everyone must state something they will do.

-- There is no judge or "check-er off" in this process. The groups needs to ask and answer honestly... "How can we help support that person?" That is the key to ongoing competency assessment.

It is not about having the answer today, but having the courage to keep asking the question to address the challenges of tomorrow."

Charge Nurse Staffing Skills Competency (Psychiatry)

This is one method to meet the Charge Nurse competency. Any unit or individual may develop a method of assessment as long is it meets the criteria for the competency and is approved by your unit education council.

PSYCHIATRY COMPETENCY

<u>To Complete the Charge Nurse Skill Worksheet</u>

• Familiarize yourself with the staffing policy attached.

• Use the worksheet to make staffing assignments for the unit illustrated.

Tips

◆ Don't make it more complex than it is. Only use information given, even if it is sketchy.

◆ In this scenario we have included the use of paraprofessionals (PA) or assigning patients to the CN.

TITLE: STAFFING ASSIGNMENTS		MANUAL: Policy Manual	
AUTHOR:	POSITION:	FILE ALPHABETICALLY IN SECTION	S
APPROVAL BODY: Director's Group	CHAIR:	REVIEW DATE:	
		REVISION DATE:	

POLICY

The Charge Nurse or Nurse Manager is responsible for patient assignment of staff. The following criteria are considered in determining staffing assignments for each shift:

a) Experience and expertise of available staff
    1) Educational preparation
    2) Qualifications of staff
    3) Orientation completed
    4) Role limitations (including clinical practice limitations of Float Pool staff, see Nursing Services policy)
b) Patient classification data
c) Patient care needs/priorities, including patient teaching and discharge planning needs
d) PCU care delivery system
e) Infection control parameters
f) Health status or limitations of staff
g) Special interests of staff
h) Availability of support/specialist resources
i) Patient requests
j) Geography of PCU

To the extent possible, an RN will make a patient assessment before delegating appropriate aspects of nursing care to ancillary personnel.

Nursing Services staff will be assigned accountability to all patients, even when nursing students are given primary assignment.

REVIEWING AUTHORITY	TITLE	DATE
REVIEWING AUTHORITY	TITLE	DATE
REVIEWING AUTHORITY	TITLE	DATE

Charge Nurse Skill Worksheet
(Psychiatry)

You are charge nurse of this Psych unit. You have 15 patients and a total of 5 staff working for day shift. Use the criteria on staffing policies and information below to make your assignments.

Patients

- Tom—28 yo, Bipolar manic, high activity, irritable.
- Molly—32 yo, Depression/ED, observe 1 hr after meals.
- James—40 yo, Depression with SI, placement issues.
- Tanya—33 yo, Depression with SI, SP, HIV positive.
- Debbie—35 yo, Psychotic Decompensation, ALDs.
- Joe—55 yo, Dangerous to self, SP, CT scan.
- Sam—18 yo, Conduct D/O, sexual prec, dope prec.
- LuAnn—50 yo, Paranoid Schiz, med adjustment, actively hallucinating.
- Dick—55 yo, Depression, cooperative/discharge.
- Richard—49, Failure outpatient treatment, SIB, la wound with drsg changes.
- Brian—28 yo, Danger to self.
- David—45 yo, Depression, ECT, confused.
- Lynne—65 yo, Para Schiz/Dementia/R/O organic, confused, help with ALL ADLS.
- Kathy—34 yo, Depression, very withdrawn, suicidal.
- Wendy—20 yo, Depression, Dissociative D/O.
- 1st Admit—unknown.

Staff

- Sally—Charge Nurse.
- Sue—Unit staff, 1 yr on unit, 10 yrs experience, pregnant.
- Nancy—Unit staff, 4 yrs experience.
- Wendy—RN from float pool.
- Larry—unit PA with 2 yrs experience.

Also Assign

- Medications to one nurse (8a-12n).
- Roves (each hour) include 15" checks.
- Team meeting at 10a and 11a.
- Food monitor, breakfast (7:30a) and lunch (12n).
- Goal group, 9am.
- Support grp, 1pm.

Indicate Patient Assignments

Sally, charge	Sue, RN	Nancy, RN	Wendy, RN	Larry, PA

Other Duties

_____ has successfully demonstrated the appropriate use of staff criteria to match patient care requirements with nursing personnel skill levels.

_____   _____
Date   Competency Reviewer

Charge Nurse Staffing Skills
Psychiatry Competency Answers

1.   The following patients must be assigned to a **nurse:** Molly, Tanya, Sam, LuAnn, Dick, David, Kathy, Wendy

2.   Tasks should be shared.
       Med cannot be with Food
       Food cannot be with Goal
       Team cannot be with Support Group

3.   Roves cannot conflict with other tasks.

4.   All PA patients should be co-assigned or PA co-assigned to a nurse.

Presentations

Presentations can be used to measure any of the three skill domains.

As many educators know, to teach someone else a concept, you must first understand it yourself. Using presentations is a valid way to measure competency of the presenter's knowledge of the subject. Most educators would say you have to know the subject pretty well to teach it to other people.

By using presentations as a verification method, you promote individual mastery of the information, as well as introduce the information to other individuals. This creates an environment in which the sharing of information is valued and rewarded.

Usually individuals are asked to share information they have gained from experience or from a recent educational event (such as a conference). Some individuals when asked to present will hesitate, either because they don't feel comfortable carrying out this type of activity, or because it seems too time consuming. If you suggest that this activity can verify a competency, it is often the stimulus people need to do a presentation. As one individual once said, "It's like killing two birds with one stone."

Because not everyone will be able to do a presentation to verify competency on a specific topic, you will need to provide other verification methods for those who do not present. Make sure that the presenter is not also required to complete the other designated competency verification methods. This defeats the purpose and stimulation for choosing presentation as a competency verification method.

Note: This verification category refers to *giving* a presentation, not merely attending a class. Just *attending* a class, inservice, or presentation does not provide a measurement for competency assessment. For a class or inservice to be used as a measurement for competency assessment, the class must include one of the other strategies listed in this guide (for example, post-test, group discussion, case study, and so on).

Continuing Medical Education Activity

Nov. 5th, 8:30-9:30 am
Medical Center Lecture Hall

Tumor Board Case Studies

Objective: *At the conclusion of the activity, the participant will be able to:*

1) List diagnostic tests necessary to diagnose cancers based on appropriate history and physical exam
2) Identify the stage of the cancer based on the results of diagnostic study.
3) Identify accepted treatment and recognize investigational protocols for various cancer therapies.
4) List and apply ancillary services available for cancer patients using a multi-disciplinary approach
5) Explain modalities available for pain control

Method: Case Discussion/Lecture Presentation

Moderator: Dr. J. G. Dupret

Patient	Surgical #	Diagnosis
A. G.	S-0907-97	37 y.o. female with skin tumor of the back
H. Z.	S-0916-97	60 y.o. male with neck mass

The Medical Center designates this educational activity for a maximum of one hour in category 1 credit towards the AMA Physician recognition award. Each physician should claim only those hours of credit that he/she actually spent in the educational activity.

Mock Events/Surveys

Mock events can be used to measure any of the three skill domains.

Mock events are simulations of real-world situations. They are carried out either in the work setting or in an artificial laboratory (such as a skills lab). Mock events are meant to create an educational and assessment activity to measure human response to stimuli. This is often used for events that are high-risk, time-dependent, infrequent, or hazardous. Here are a few examples of mock events:

- Mock codes
- Simulated disaster drills or other emergency situations
- Mock surveys for accreditation or inspection agencies
- Mock drills (such as fire, severe weather, power outages)
- Hazardous material spill clean-ups
- Mock surveys of proper equipment use and maintenance

Mock events must reflect individual performance. You cannot conduct a mock event in a work setting and conclude that all employees in that area are competent to perform those skills. Only those individuals who participate in the mock event may be validated.

Debriefing sessions following a mock event are an essential element. You will get more out of a mock event by reflecting on the actions that were taken during the event. It also helps deal with some of the anxieties the event may have produced. Recognizing mistakes and identifying actions to take next time are an essential part of ongoing learning and development. Make that a part of your next mock event.

Debriefing sessions are also very appropriate following real-world disasters and stressful events. The sessions can serve to assess actions taken in the actual event.

Example:

Use a debriefing session after your next code to assess the roles carried out by each person and the group communication and problem solving. This can identify whether job functions were carried out in an appropriate manner, or if team behaviors helped or hindered the outcomes.

Spend some time reviewing the steps taken and communication strategies used after your organization has responded to a disaster or severe weather situation. Look for ways to improve performance, as well as reward effort. Debriefing strategies have been shown to decrease anxieties and increase confidence for future action.

130   *Chapter 4*

Quality Improvement Monitors

Quality improvement monitors can be used to measure any of the three skill domains.

Quality improvement (QI) monitors are common tools we use to monitor the environment and the outcomes for our customers. QI monitors are often used to check compliance with policies and protocols, as well as to benchmark desired outcomes and the successful achievement of these outcomes.

QI monitors give us valuable information about the progress and performance of the organization. These tools can also be useful in verifying competencies of individuals. Many of the QI tools we use to assess overall organizational performance start by collecting data on individual performance. Here are some examples of where QI monitors may be used for individual performance. You probably already have these monitors in place to measure overall outcomes.

- Chart/Documentation audits
- Compliance with Infection Control policies
- Appropriate equipment set-up/teardown/clean-up

One thing to always keep in mind when using QI monitors for competency assessment: The QI monitor must reflect *individual* performance. You cannot monitor 10% of the group and conclude from the data that all of the group is competent in that area. The monitor must reflect an individual's performance.

Because most QI monitors are not designed to capture the performance of every employee, just a sample, you will need to have more than one way for the group to verify competencies. A QI monitor can be offered as one of the verification methods to assess an identified competency. As mentioned before, giving people more than one option is very valuable. This reflects many of the concepts of adult learning. By allowing individuals to choose their competency verification methods, you increase accountability and show respect for the individuals.

Choosing a competency for which QI monitoring is a competency verification can also have an impact on your QI program. Selecting a QI monitor as a verification method encourages people to be a part of the QI process. It may even be the impetus that gets some people involved in QI who never were before.

Using QI monitors as a competency verification tool can benefit both your competency assessment process and your quality improvement process. It has a great deal of potential. Give it a try.

Example:

Here is one example of how an organization used a QI monitor to assess skills in the Documentation of Patient Education.

This organization's leadership had a great deal of QI data showing that they were not documenting patient education. They created a competency around this issue and decided to use their QI monitor as a verification method for this competency.

They modified their Patient Education Documentation QI monitor to reflect not only that documentation was done correctly, but who did it. Making this change allowed the data to reflect individual performance and skill. Then each staff member was asked to use the QI data to demonstrate that he or she successfully completed patient education each quarter. This required the employee to go to the QI log book and look for his or her name each quarter.

A few benefits from this process:

- *The employees became familiar with the QI log book.*
- *Employees realized that they needed to document patient education in order to be captured in the QI data, so they started to do more accurate documentation.*

- *Seeing other colleagues on the QI log book accomplishing successful documentation tended to create a bit of good competition to also do better documentation.*

   Overall, this competency approach helped this organization improve individual skills associated with patient education documentation, as well as providing a few other benefits along the way.

FORM
Quality
Improvement
Monitor

UBBST
Observation
Quality Improvement Data Collection Form

Area: _____   Data Collector: _____   Employee: _____

Guidelines for Data Retrieval: Observe staff during procedures and every day practice. Score a positive for technique that is in compliance with the indicator. Score a negative if not in compliance.

KEY
+ Met Indicator
- Did not meet
NA Not Applicable

Indicators	+	-	NA	expected	Remarks
1. Employee wore gloves to touch any body substance (blood, stool, drainage, etc.)				100%	
2. Employee wore gloves to touch any item, bed clothes, or skin visibly soiled with body substances.				100%	
3. Employee wore gloves to touch non-intact skin of patient and/or to protect their own non-intact skin.				100%	
4. Employee wore a gown when they anticipated clothing might become soiled with body substances.				100%	
5. Employee wore a mask during any procedure that they anticipated body substances might splash or spray.				100%	
6. Employee wore protective eyewear during any procedure that they anticipated body substances might splash or spray. (personal glasses need solid side shields, permanently affixed.)				100%	
7. Employee washed their hands after removing gloves.				100%	
8. Employee discarded needles and other sharp instruments in a puncture-resistant container.				100%	
9. Employee did not recap dirty needles.					

Other pertinent Data (i.e., Room #)

98

Notes

Notes

Chapter Five

Developing a Successful Competency Assessment Process

- Age-specific aspects of competency assessment
- Developing a competency program that promotes accountability
- Consequences/Managers' responses to competency problems
- Documenting and tracking the competency process

Age-Specific Aspects

Many skills and abilities are necessary for us to successfully meet our customers' needs. Understanding the age-specific aspects of our customers is essential for us to apply our skills to meet our customers' varied needs. This section will address some of the ways to think about assessing this aspect of skill in your competency program without making it an overwhelming, monotonous part of the process.

First, you *should* assess age-specific aspects in your competency assessment program, but that does not mean you must have a separate age-specific competency each year. No regulatory standards require your organization to show an age-specific video every year, or complete age-specific checklists on each employee. Although such actions may comply with some regulatory standards, this approach also can send a message to your employees that your competency program is based on satisfying regulatory standards, and not on meeting the needs of your organization. Overall, this approach works against building a meaningful philosophy for competency assessment.

When identifying the competencies for each job class, do not automatically create an age-specific competency each assessment period. Select the competencies you will require each period based on the competency worksheet in Chapter 2. This worksheet identifies competencies based on what's "new, changing, high-risk, and problematic." Develop a separate age-specific competency only if it comes up as an item when you complete the worksheet.

Assessing age-specific aspects does not mean you have to have a free-standing age-specific competency. Instead it is easier and more meaningful to include age-specific items in the other competencies you identify through the competency worksheet.

Example: Through the competency worksheet, your group identifies a new "customer population you are starting to care for—diabetics. Your group develops a case study to measure the skills and knowledge that the staff should have to treat insulin reactions. The case study describes a 37-year-old patient who is experiencing many symptoms. Questions in the case study ask about the staff's response to her symptoms. The last question asks, "Would you do anything different if this was an 87-year-old woman?" (See the Case Study section of Chapter 4 for a sample of this diabetes case study with an age-specific twist.)

You have now included age-specific aspects into your already identified competencies. This approach can often be more realistic and meaningful for staff and better for your overall competency program.

A stand-alone age-specific competency can be great during orientation when you are first introducing employees to the needs of their customers, but repetition of such competencies can become monotonous and meaningless over time. The best approach is to add the age-specific aspect to other competency needs identified each competency period. Never create a competency just to comply with a regulatory standard. This approach is too destructive to your overall program, and has never motivated staff to increase their participation or ownership in the competency process.

As you create any competency, make it meaningful and applicable to the group that is required to complete it. This means that you should avoid "one size fits all" competencies. For example, it makes little sense to have the environmental services workers watch an age-specific video describing how toddlers learn and then take a test to measure their skills on age. This may provide an accurate measurement, but it will probably not mean much to the environmental service workers. They may ask, "How does knowing 'how toddlers learn best' help me do my job?"

A better approach: As part of a recent staff meeting for environmental services, we included on the agenda an opportunity to review the recent changes in cleaning products for the year. We identified that we would be going over the hazardous material information for these new cleaning products and the best ways to use them. These are typical competencies often identified in custodial jobs.

We decided to use a question/answer session and discussion group to assess this competency. After describing the new chemicals and their hazards, we asked the group several questions about the cleaning products. During the session we asked, "You normally work in an adult area, but one day you are asked to clean a public or pediatric area. Would you organize your cart differently that day?"

We had several good answers. One participant said, "I would take all my dangerous chemicals and put them on the top of my cart out of reach of little fingers." Another person said, "I would go one step further than that. I would put all my dangerous chemicals on the top of the cart in a carry-all bucket. When I went on my break, I would take the bucket with me, so none of the dangerous stuff would be left behind unattended."

This is a much more meaningful way to incorporate age-specific aspects into the competency process—one the employees can understand and more easily accept. It is much better than requiring an age-specific competency because "JCAHO says we have to do it." Don't you agree?

The Key to a Successful Competency Assessment

The Manager's Response and Follow-up to Competency Assessment

Managers set the tone and create an environment that supports individual accountability for competency assessment. The manager's response to the competency process will establish the overall philosophy of the competency program for the future. *Policies* will not create support for the competency process. *Leadership actions* will.

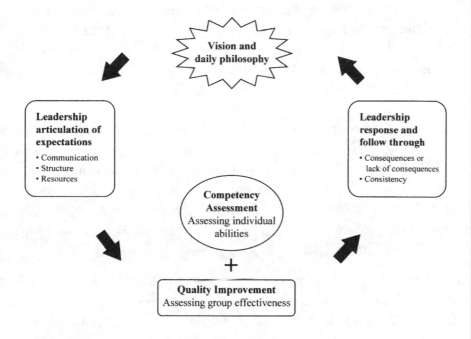

Articulating competency expectations

Leaders and managers will articulate the expectations of the competency process through their communication, structures that are established to support competency assessment, and resources that are dedicated to the process. Employees cannot successfully complete the competency process, unless they clearly understand the expectations. We need to help managers develop creative ways to articulate the competency process to all employees. This includes articulation of the employee's accountability in the competency process. Managers should not *do* the competency assess process *for* the employee. Instead managers should clearly define the process and how the employees can meet the competency assessment requirements.

Establishing consequences

The most critical element to the success of your competency assessment process is the consequences and follow-up demonstrated by managers when employees do not successfully complete the process. The consequences (or lack of consequences) will create the new philosophy around your competency program.

Many leaders are surprised that their employees do not take the process seriously, or that they do not actually accept accountability. I usually ask, "What happens if they don't do their competencies?" If the answer is, "Nothing," then do not be surprised if your program is unsuccessful.

Defining consequences

Most people can think of only one consequence for individuals who do not successfully complete their competencies, and that is to fire them. But you have so many more choices than that. Because there are many different situations and responses people may have to the competency process, managers need many different types of responses.

One of the best ways to come up with a variety of approaches to employee behavior is to discuss options with other managers. By sharing possible situations with peers, you can collect a variety of possible consequences for the situations you discuss. Also ask yourself what motivates *you* to do *your* work or to take responsible actions. Creative consequences may be more obvious than you think.

Consequences can be put in place long before competencies are due. I like to have consequences that motivate posi-

tive behavior in the competencies process in place throughout the year.

Example: *As I mentioned before, I like to give employees a
variety of options to validate their competencies. For example,
we may have a competency with four options—things such as
case study/discussion group, skill fair return demos (with a
pizza party afterwards), games and puzzle session, or read-
ing the policy and taking a test. I set up the activities for the
year so that the fun activities start to disappear as the year
goes on. If employees wait until the end of the year to finally
do their competency, then the only choice they may have left
is to "read the policy and take the test."*

*This approach sends the message that if you get motivated
early or you participate with the group during the "compe-
tency-of-the-month time," you will have more fun than if you
wait until the last minute. This becomes a consequence—one
that rewards positive behavior and discourages negative
behavior.*

Incorporating Competency Assessment in Daily Operations

As always, start with your vision. Ask yourself with every effort your organization pursues, "What are we trying to achieve?" As you begin a new initiative or change, start with education. Allow for some implementation and application time. Then use a quality improvement (Ql) monitor to assess the progress of the initiative or change. The results from QI data will indicate whether implementation was successful. If the data indicates a problem, you can at that point develop a competency that reflects this need.

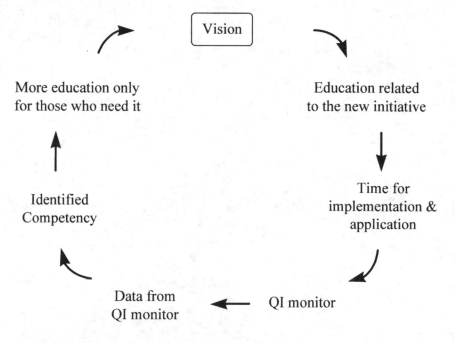

This approach is not only cost effective, but it also streamlines competency assessment to the skills actually needed in a given situation. For example, what is actually preventing employees from achieving a desired outcome may not be lack of a technical skill (such as following a procedure), but lack of an attitudinal skill (such as consistently applying the skills they have in all situations). The skill of handwashing is a perfect example. It is not that employees do not know how to wash their hands; the problem is that they do not have the attitude or mind-set to apply that skill every day.

If you approached this skill with a competency first, rather than with QI, you would probably focus on developing a technical skill competency. If you do the QI first, you would uncover the real problem. The problem is not a lack of technical skill, but a lack of attitudinal skill.

After the competency is identified, focus on the skill required, not the education at this point. Only use education for those individuals who need it—those who are having difficulty achieving the identified competency. This is a much more cost-effective approach.

Malcolm Knowles (1970) stated, "A learning need is the gap between the learner's present level of competence and a higher level of performance which is defined by the learner, the organization, or society." Learning or education is not the required element—the competency expectation is the required element. If people have the skill already, then education is not required. Only those who fall short of the expectation may need the education.

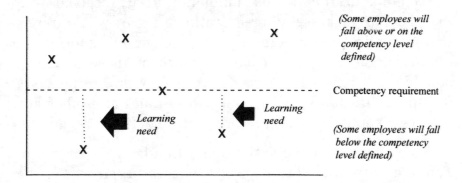

Documenting and Tracking

As the manager verifies competency achievement for each individual, some type of competency assessment summary should be sent to a central location for overall organizational documentation and tracking. This does not need to be the original individual competency assessment tool. The original competency assessment tools and documents can be kept wherever they are most useful to the employee, manager, and organization. These forms should be kept only as long as the manager and employee need them to verify competency assessment and support any plan for improvement. After that, they can be tossed.

The minimum that needs to be kept and archived is:

- a summary of employees who were deemed competent or not

- the action plans associated with those areas that fell short of expectations

- one original copy of the competencies for each area each competency period and examples of the verification methods (paper copy or on computer disc)

The organization can use tabulation forms received from managers to track overall organizational progress and trends that may arise. Some examples of these summary forms are found on the next few pages. Reports of these activities should then be given to executives, your governing body (board of directors, trustees, and so on) and any other key leaders accountable for monitoring organizational progress.

Tracking competency assessment trends in the organization is an essential element to the successful growth of the organization. Collecting and reviewing trends of the aggregate data is required by many regulatory groups (such as

JCAHO). This analysis of trends is also essential for organizational survival and strategic planning. It makes good business sense.

FORM
Competency
Tabulation

Supervisor Competency Tabulation

Supervisor _____ Dept./Work area _____

Please indicate the competency status and date completed (or reviewed) for all the employees you supervise.

Competency Status: *COMP* = Competencies successfully validated
                      NYDC = Employee is Not Yet Deemed Competent

                      NYDC can be used for employees who...
                      ♦ are on leave
                      ♦ have not successfully verified all their competencies
                      ♦ fail to turn in completed competency forms

                      An action plan must be identified for each employee given an NYDC status.

Employee	Date completed	Competency Status

Return to Human Resources _____ by _____

Supervisor Competency Evaluation

We would like to track issues and trends related to competency assessment. As you compile information regarding each of your employees, please note the following:

What difficulties did employees have in successfully completing competencies:

What worked well in the competency process:

Was there any competency that was difficult for the employees to achieve:

Were there any issues relating to the communication of the competency process:

Was competency support available to you and your staff when you needed it:

Please return to _____ by _____.   Thank you!

FORM
Competency
Evaluation

Notes

Notes

Chapter Six

Competency Assessment and Performance Appraisal

- The difference between competency assessment and performance review

- Defining the overlap between the two processes

- Combining the two processes, or keeping them separate

Competency Assessment and Performance Review

Competency assessment and performance review can be combined as one process or kept separate. Whichever approach is taken, look for overlap and duplication between the two processes. Take some time to select the appropriate evaluation for each process.

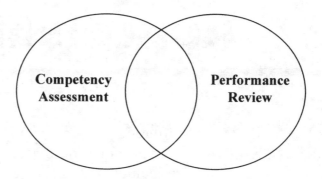

Performance review has a great deal of overlap with competency assessment because of the way it has evolved over time. Performance review usually attempts to evaluate interpersonal and critical thinking aspects of the job, often because our competency programs focus mostly on technical skills. This approach does not capture all the skills needed to carry out the job, so we stick the other skills (interpersonal and critical thinking) in performance review—not because it is the most effective way to assess those aspects, but because we know they are important, so we must put them somewhere.

A better approach is to include the domains of critical thinking and interpersonal skills in the competency process, not in performance review. Performance review often relies on the manager's observation and assessment to make judgments concerning these skills. As discussed in earlier chapters, this approach usually is not effective.

Competency assessment addresses the dynamic nature of the job. Your competency assessment process should demonstrate this by developing competencies that reflect your organization's quality improvement efforts, other problematic areas, and new and changing aspects of the environment. This means competencies should be developed each year (or assessment period) to reflect those dynamic aspects. Avoid repeating the same competencies each year. This does not create a dynamic process of assessment. Individuals very rarely lose skills and abilities they have acquired; more often the skills required to do the job change, and individuals may not have the skills needed to meet these new demands. By using a dynamic process of competency assessment, you can make competency assessment a more meaningful and effective activity in your organization.

Competency assessment is the process of providing ongoing review of the skills needed to carry out various job functions. Because competency assessment is an ongoing, dynamic process, it will constantly change to meet the demands of the healthcare environment. Competency assessment should look different in each organization and for each job class in that organization.

Although competency assessment shares some characteristics with performance review, it is a different process.

Competency assessment looks at

- the knowledge, skills, abilities, and behaviors needed to carry out job functions.

Its primary purpose is to make sure the organization has the right person doing the right job.

Performance review, although it may cover some of the same territory as competency assessment, has as its main objectives

- to review the employee's adherence to contractual agreements/organizational policies

- to evaluate the employee's achievement of criteria to keep or advance in a given role

- and sometimes to determine the amount of compensation for that effort.

Competency assessment and performance review share common elements, but also have distinct differences. The following diagram shows some of these differences by describing the unique purpose of each. Some examples of these elements are given in the circles below.

Performance Review

Unique purpose: *Assure that employee is fulfilling contractual agreements of job and following organizational policies.*

Review based on:

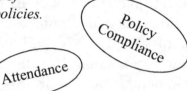

- ◆ Organizational Policies

- ◆ Professional Practice Standards

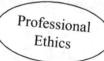

- ◆ Job Description

Competency Assessment

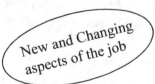

Unique purpose: *Assess the ongoing skills needed to address the changing nature of the job.*

Assessment based on:

- ◆ Ongoing competencies identified for each job class

The form on the following pages provides an example of ways to combine these two processes. You do not have to combine the two processes, but this form may help you understand the key aspects of each process. Then you can make better decisions about what approach you feel will best meet your organizational needs.

Section 1 reflects the unique purpose of performance review. This reviews the contractual compliance the employee has with the organization. This section is carried out by the supervisor all through the year. If the employee fails to comply with policies and expectations, the supervisor needs to address these issues. Managers do not wait until the performance review to deal with these issues. They are usually addressed at the time of the breach in compliance. Section 1 reflects this process of reviewing compliance and reminds us to document the action plans needed.

Generally, this section is only filled in if there is a lack of compliance. We would not write down every expectation (or policy) and check off that an individual complied with it during the year. However, some performance review forms start to take on this type of approach—getting longer and longer every year.

Section 2 reflects the competency assessment process as described throughout this text. The employee is accountable for verifying his or her identified competencies throughout the year. So this section will be given to the employee to complete, and then returned to the supervisor at the end of the competency period.

Section 3 provides a way to document the annual requirements of the job. This can include retraining that is required each year, required educational events, and current licensure and registration evidence. This section is also carried out by the employee, and the data is brought to the supervisor when completed.

Sections 1, 2. and 3 all come down to a "Yes or No" answer. These first three sections do not reflect a three-tier response such as "Does not meet, Meets, or Exceeds

Expectations." For example, you cannot comply with a policy, or "REALLY" comply with a policy. You can't be competent or really competent. These three sections all reflect an evaluation that comes down to Yes or No.

Section 4 is the one that can reflect the "exceeds expectations" aspects of the job. It is much better to separate this from sections 1, 2, and 3. This makes it clearer for the employee and the supervisor.

Section 4 can be used to recognize the employee's behavior and performance that exceeds the expectations noted in the competencies or performance standards identified. This section can also be used to help plan a personal development plan that the employee may want to focus on and may need the organization's support to achieve. This gives both the employee and the supervisor an opportunity to look at goals for the future, and the efforts needed to achieve those goals.

FORM
Combining
Performance
Appraisal and
Competency
Assessment

Combining Performance Appraisal and Competency Assessment

1. Standards of Performance   *(filled out by the supervisor)*

This employee has adhered to the contractual expectations of the job as described in the...

❑ Organizational policies   ❑ Performance standards
❑ Job description   ❑ Professional practice
                                                      standards

❑ Yes   ❑ No   *(If no, please indicate the action plan below)*

2. Competency Assessment   *(filled out by the employee throughout the year)*

Competencies	*Methods of Verification*	*Date Completed*
Technical Domain		
Critical Thinking Domain		
Interpersonal Domain		

An abbreviated version of a form combining competency assessment and performance review

3. Annual Requirements   *(filled out by the employee*
                                            throughout the year)

❑ Licensure/registration current   Exp. date _____

Annual Retraining	*Methods of Education*	*Date Completed*
Infection Control (OSHA)		
Life Support (CPR)		
Chemical Hazards (OSHA)		
Life Safety		

This person has been assessed, and is competent to perform as a
_____ in _____.

❑ Yes   ❑ No, not yet deemed competent.
                    (If no, complete action plan below)

Action Plan:

4. Recognition and   *(filled out by the employee*
  Personal Development   *and/or supervisor)*

This section can be used to recognize those employee behaviors and
performance that exceeded expectations. This section can also be
used to plan a personal development plan that the employee may want
to focus on and may need the organization's support to achieve.

Notes

Notes

Appendix

Leadership Competencies

Through the following leadership competencies, we are working together to move toward strategies that help our organizational as a whole move forward to meet its goals. As leaders we are each responsible to reflect on our contribution and demonstrate the leadership skills required to build organizational adaptability to respond to the ever-changing demands of healthcare today.

COMPETENCY STATEMENT	VERIFICATION METHODS (SELECT ONE FOR EACH COMPETENCY)
Customer Focus Demonstrates the ability to apply customer service principles to the everyday work situation.	❑ Select two peers/staff to complete the Customer Service Peer Review ❑ Complete the Customer Service Exemplar
Dealing with Ambiguity Demonstrates the ability to deal with ambiguity, change, and chaos in this dynamic environment of healthcare.	❑ Select two peers/staff to complete the "Dealing with Ambiguity" Peer Review Worksheet
Dealing with Paradox Demonstrates the leadership ability to find the balance in daily situations that represent a paradox.	❑ Give a group presentation to your peers demonstrating how you or your group has dealt with a paradox. (Use the Paradox Exemplar form as a guide) ❑ Complete the "Dealing with Paradox" Exemplar
Learning on the Fly Demonstrates the ability to learning on the fly and making learning a part of your daily leadership behaviors.	❑ Complete the "Learning on the Fly" Case Studies ❑ Complete the "Learning on the Fly" Exemplar
Managing Vision and Purpose Demonstrates the ability to translate the organizational vision and goals into daily actions for you and your team.	❑ Complete the "Managing the Vision" Mapping Worksheet
Total Quality Improvement Demonstrates active leadership the QI process by carrying out quality improvement activities.	❑ Submit a summary of a current QI project you or your group is doing to support creating quality products and services in our organization

<table>
<tr><td colspan="2" align="center">*Possible competencies for*
Office Specialists/Secretaries/Support Staff</td></tr>
</table>

Competency Statemement	*Method of verification*
Task Prioritization/Time Management: Appropriately and efficiently identifies, prioritizes, and follows through on assignments.	❑ Peer review/customer review ❑ Supervisor review
Phone triage: Demonstrates the ability to appropriately direct phone calls and requests to meet customers needs	❑ Peer review ❑ On phone customer survey
Room scheduling: Assigns rooms to meet departmental and interdepartmental needs	❑ Peer Reveiw ❑ QI monitor
Data Entry: Accurate and timely entry of data into computer documentation system	❑ Observation of daily work ❑ QI monitor
Mazimizes the use of existing computer software	❑ Peer review ❑ Observation of daily work
Dealing with people: Demontrates knowledge of dealing with difficult people.	❑ Attends inservice on people skills and completes test or group activity successfully
Applies principles of dealing with difficult people over the phone or in person	❑ Exemplar ❑ Peer review
Word Processing: Demonstrates the ability to create memos, letters, and other documents using ____ software.	❑ Observation of daily work ❑ Production of document itself

FORM
Dietary
Competencies

Possible competencies for
Dietary

<u>**Competency Statement**</u>	<u>**Method of verification**</u>
<u>Food Service worker:</u> Demonstrates the ability to follow a recipe for food preparation	❑ Return demonstration ❑ Observation of daily work
Demonstrates the skill required to handle a customer, patient, or family member who has a complaint.	❑ Case Study/ Role play ❑ Observation of daily work ❑ Exemplar
Successfully demonstrates safe use of the *(new equipment.)*	❑ Return demonstration ❑ Observation of daily work
Demonstrates a basic understanding of safe food preparation and handling, and the health risks associated with breach on policy.	❑ Post-test ❑ Video and discussion group exercise ❑ Presentation to peers

---

Possible competencies for
Staff Development Specialists

Competency Statememt	Method of verification
Manages use of educational resources in the most cost effective way.	❑ Exemplar ❑ Peer review
Demonstrates role modeling of a healthy learning environment.	❑ Program evaluations from educational activities ❑ Peer Review
Mentors staff in how to creating, facilitating, and evaluating educational activities	❑ Peer Reveiw ❑ Signature from staff member mentored
Applies critical thinking to interactions to increase effectiveness as an educator.	❑ Observation of daily work ❑ Peer review exemplar
Applies the principles of adult learning to all educational situations.	❑ Program evaluations from educational activities ❑ Exemplar ❑ Peer review
Assists effectiveness of groups and teams through group facilitation and education.	❑ Peer Review from groups assisted ❑ Exemplar
Demonstrates the ability to act as a internal consultant to assist groups in assessing a given situation for its true problematic nature.	❑ Peer Review ❑ Consultation Evaluation

Possible competencies for
Staff Development Specialists

Competency Statemement	Method of verification
Demostrates knowledge of the basic principles of (selected educational or staff development theory)	❑ Attend an educational event, or read about a theory, and then present what you have learned. ❑ Exemplar of application of theory into a real life situationn

FORM
Chief Financial
Officer and
Business
Coordinators
Competencies

Possible competencies for
Chief Financial Officer & Business Coordinators

Competency Statement	_Method of verification_
Creates a fiscal tracking system that provides usable fiscal data to organizational leaders	❑ Observation of daily practice (Existence of system) ❑ Peer leader evaluation
Provides expertise and education in reading and interpreting fiscal data.	❑ Evaluation from individuals or groups assisted ❑ Peer Review
Demonstrates timely communication of significant fiscal changes to leadership staff.	❑ Peer Review from leadership staff ❑ Signature from several leadership staff
Demonstrates the use of appropriate fiscal tracking and documentation	❑ Mock audits ❑ Actual audits

*Possible competencies for
VP of Patient Care Services
or Director of Nursing*

Competency Statement	Method of verification
Creates a philosophy of patient care and a model for care delivery.	❑ Submission of actual written documents or policies
Demonstrates the ability to communicate the departmental goals to all managers and staff.	❑ Peer review or evaluation representative of all departmental of employees
Demonstrates fiscal accountability for department resources.	❑ Fiscal management data ❑ Exemplar detailing strategies of fiscal accountability
Provides leadership and guidance to other leaders and managers in goal setting, problem solving, resource management, and outcome achievement	❑ Peer review by leaders and managers
Demonstrates a commitment to a healthy work environment by modeling the desired behaviors and encouraging these in others	❑ Peer Review from anyone with whom you interact ❑ Signature from anyone employee who see this competency in action
Demonstrates the ability to cope with and manage change, as well as help others do the same	❑ Self assessment ❑ Peer assessment

Possible competencies for
VP of Patient Care Services
or Director of Nursing

Competency Statement	Method of verification
Collaborates with other departments to create systems and problem solve ongoing issues that impact care delivery.	❑ Peer review from peers in other departments ❑ Exemplar outlining collaboration efforts
Incorporates patient satisfaction data and quality improvement data into departmental care delivery goals.	❑ Exemplar ❑ Written documentation of goals identified
Demonstrates a clear understanding of regulations applicable to patient care (i.e. JCAHO Standards, State Nursing Practice Act, etc.)	❑ Observation of daily practice ❑ Articulation of understanding through presentation of information

Possible competencies for
CEO or Director

Competency Statement	Method of verification
Creates a vision, philosophy, and mission statement for the organization.	❑ Submission of actual written documents
Demonstrates the ability to communicate the organizational vision, philosophy, mission, and/or goals to all levels of employees.	❑ Peer review or evaluation representative of all levels of employees
Provides leadership and guidance to other leaders and managers in goal setting, problem solving, resource management, and outcome achievement	❑ Overall review of strategic planning and other processes ❑ Peer Review by leaders and managers
Demonstrates a commitment to a healthy work environment by modeling the desired behaviors and encouraging these in others	❑ Peer Review from anyone with whom you interact ❑ Signature from any employee who see this competency in action
Demonstrates the ability to cope with and manage change, as well as help others do the same	❑ Self assessment ❑ Peer assessment
Demonstrates the ability to achieve outcomes within allocated resources	❑ Fiscal management data ❑ Exemplar detailing strategies of fiscal accountability

References and Suggested Resources

1997 Accreditation Manual for Hospitals. Volume 1—Standards, Volume 2—Scoring Guidelines. Joint Commission on Accreditation of Healthcare Organizations. One Renaissance Blvd. Oakbrook Terrace, IL 60181 Phone: (708) 916-5600.

Andrew, Cook, Davidson, Schurman, Taylor, and Wensel. (1994). *Organizational Transformation in Health Care.* San Francisco: Jossey-Bass Publishers.

Blanchard, Carlos, and Randolph. (1996). *Empowerment Takes More Than a Minute.* San Francisco: Berrett-Koehler Publishers.

Bellman G. (1992). *Getting Things Done When You Are Not in Charge.* NY: Simon and Schuster.

Benner, P. (1982). "Issues in Competency Based Testing." *Nursing Outlook.* pp. 303–309.

Connors, R., Smith, T., and Hickman, C. (1994). *The Oz Principle.* Englewood, NJ: Prentice Hall.

del Bueno, Barker, and Christmyer. (1980). "Implementing a competency-based orientation program." *Nurse Educator.* May/June, pp. 16–20.

del Bueno, Reeves Griffin, Burke, and Foley. (1990). "The Clinical Teacher: A Critical Link to Competence Development." *Journal of Nursing Staff Development,* Vol. 6, No. 3, May/June 1990, pp. 135–138.

Fournies, F. (1988). *Why Employees Don't Do What They're Supposed To Do.* Liberty Hall Press/McGraw Hill, Inc.

Fulton, R. (1988). *Common Sense Supervision.* Berkley, CA: Ten Speed Press.

Gaucher, E. and Coffey, R. (1990). *Transforming Healthcare Organizations.* San Francisco: Jossey-Bass Publishers.

Gaucher, E. and Coffey, R. (1993). *Total Quality in Healthcare.* San Francisco: Jossey-Bass Publishers.

Goleman, Daniel. (1995). *Emotional Intelligence.* NY: Bantam Books.

Gustafson, M. (1996). *The Educator's Guide to Teaching Methodologies.* Minneapolis, MN: Creative HealthCare Management.

Hakim. C. (1994). *We Are All Self-Employed.* San Francisco: Berrett-Koehler Publishers.

Howard, R. (editor). (1993). *The Learning Imperative.* Boston: Harvard Business Review.

Hyland and Yost. (1994). *Reflections for Managers.* NY: McGraw-Hill.

Jeska, S. and Fischer, K. (1996). *Performance Improvement in Staff Development: The Next Evolution.* Pensacola, FL: NNSDO.

Kissler, G. (1996). *Leading the Health Care Revolution.* Chicago: American College of Healthcare Executives.

Knowles, M. (1988). *The Modem Practice of Adult Education: From pedagogy to andragogy.* Chicago: Association Press, Follet Publishing Company.

Kreitzer, Wright, Hamlin, Towey, Marko, & Disch. (1997). "Creating a Healthy Work Environment in the Midst of Organizational Change and Transition." *Journal of Nursing Administration.* June 1997.

Manthey, M. *Commitment to My Coworker* (1994). Minneapolis, MN: Creative Healthcare Management.

McLagan, P. & Nel, C. (1995). *The Age of Participation.* San Francisco: Berrett-Koehler Publishers.

Miller and Babcock. (1996). *Critical Thinking Applied to Nursing.* St. Louis: Mosby.

Nair, K. (1994). *A Higher Standard of Leadership.* San Francisco: Berrett-Koehler Publishers.

Nelson, B. (1994). *1001 Ways to Reward Employees.* NY: Workman Publishing.

Owenby, P. (1992). "Making Case Studies Come Alive." *Training.* January, 1992.

Pollock, M.B. (1981). "Speaking of Competencies." *Health Education.* Jan/Feb 1981, pp 9–13.

Reed and Procter. (1993). *Nurse Education: A Reflextive Approach.* London: Edward Arnold

Robinson & Robinson. (1996). *Performance Consulting: Moving Beyond Training.* San Francisco: Berrett-Koehler.

Wright, D. (1996). *Creative Ways to Validate Competencies.* Video/Text. Minneapolis, MN: Creative Healthcare Resources.

Wright, D. (1996). *Tying Competency Assessment to Quality Improvement: As Easy as Riding a Bike!* Video. Minneapolis, MN: Creative Healthcare Resources.

Wright, D. (1996). *How to Create Accountability through Competency Assessment.* Video. Minneapolis, MN: Creative Healthcare Resources.

Wright, D. (1996). *How to Create and Promote Self Learning Packets.* Video. Minneapolis, MN: Creative Healthcare Resources.

Wright, D. (1997). *Secrets to Creating a Healthy Work Environment in Healthcare.* Audiotape and text. Eau Claire, WI: Professional Education Systems, Inc.

Zenger, J. (1996) *Not Just for CEOs: Sure-fire Success Secrets for the Leader in Each of Us.* Chicago: Irwin Professional Publishing.

Notes

Notes

Notes

Notes